Fairy Tales, Myths and Legends

Scholastic Children's Books
An imprint of Scholastic Ltd
Euston House, 24 Eversholt Street, London, NW1 1DB, UK
Registered office: Westfield Road, Southam, Warwickshire, CV47 0RA
SCHOLASTIC and associated logos are trademarks and/or
registered trademarks of Scholastic Inc.

First published in the UK by Scholastic Ltd, 2018

A CIP catalogue record for this book
is available from the British Library.

ISBN 978-93-5471-977-6

First edition: 2018
This reprint edition: May, 2024
Printed in India at Sai Printo Pack Pvt. Ltd.

www.scholastic.co.uk

Fairy Tales, MYTHS AND LEGENDS

SCHOLASTIC

For my dad,
thank you for the big blue book
and the best bedtime stories. My love
of books started with you.

Contents

Introduction

Fairy tales, myths and legends have existed for thousands of years, but they haven't always been written down. In their earliest forms, they were shared by spoken word. These cautionary tales were sometimes gruesome and often scary but they always came with a moral for children to take heed of, and perhaps that's why they have always been so popular with both children and grown-ups. Every well-known story has been retold by one author or another and, using early versions as inspiration, the stories in this collection are no exception. While the tales within these pages stay true to older records, they have also been rewritten specifically for children today.

The Frog Prince

The most popular version of "The Frog Prince" was written by German brothers Jacob and Wilhelm Grimm. *Children's and Household Tales*, which published in two volumes in 1812 and 1815, was one of the first known collections of its kind. The story of the frog prince has changed in small ways during its republication and has inspired many retellings, including Andrew Lang's "The Frog", which featured in *The Violet Fairy Book* that published in 1901, and a Russian version called "Tsarevna Lyagushka", which reversed the male and female roles within the tale to depict a prince who meets an enchanted female frog who is in fact a sorceress.

One peaceful evening at twilight, a young princess went walking in the woods. She soon came across a beautiful spring, whose bank she sat upon to rest awhile, and, while she rested, the princess played with her golden ball – which was her favourite plaything and most prized possession. She threw the ball into the air and caught it carefully when it fell back down towards her. Higher and higher it went, again and again.

After a time, the princess became careless and threw the golden ball so high that she failed to catch it. Instead, it sprang away from her and rolled along the ground. With an almost silent *plop!* it dropped into the spring. The princess peered into the water, but it was hopeless; her golden ball was lost. As you can imagine, she was very distraught and soon began to cry.

As she wept, a voice spoke to her, asking, "Princess, why do you weep so?"

As her eyes searched the spring, she suddenly noticed a frog poking his head from the water.

In her surprise, she cried, "My golden ball has

fallen into the spring. If I could only hold my ball again, I would give all my fine clothes and jewels, and everything that I have in the world! But you can't help me, you nasty frog."

The frog considered her words for a moment. "I do not want your fine clothes and jewels, but if you will accept me as a companion, let me eat from your plate and sleep upon your bed, then I shall bring you your golden ball."

Well, the princess agreed to the frog's request in an instant, saying, "I promise you *all* of that, if only you bring me my ball." But did she mean it? No she did not! For, truly, the selfish princess thought the frog to be rather slimy and horrid. Still, the frog did not know this, so he dived into the spring in search of the princess's beloved ball. It did not take him long to find it, and with triumph he swam through the water and presented it to the princess – who was so happy to be reunited with her sparkly possession that she immediately forgot about her promise to the frog and instead rushed straight back to the castle to share her delight with her family.

"Wait!" called the frog, as she hurried away. "Take me with you!" But the princess wasn't listening.

The next day, as the royal family sat down to dinner, they were interrupted by a noise at the castle door. Someone was calling for the princess.

"My dear princess, please hear me now,
Do not break your solemn vow.
By the spring where you did flee,
You promised you would cherish me."

It was the frog! He had followed the princess to the castle. Of course, she had forgotten all about him and was rather annoyed that he was there, right outside the castle door. She tried to ignore him, but it was no use. The frog continued to call for her.

"Who on earth is that?" asked her father the king, and she had to tell him the truth. The king was an honourable man, and on hearing his daughter's tale he was quite stern with her.

"If you have made a promise, you must keep it," he said. "Go – open the door, allow the frog to enter the castle."

The princess did what her father asked, and as she walked back into the dining room she was followed by the distinct *squelch-squelch* sound of the frog hopping across the marble floor behind her.

She sat back down at the table and resumed her meal, sulkily. But before she had taken a mouthful, the frog called up to her from the floor.

"Please, Princess, lift me on to the chair so that I may sit next to you," he said.

So the princess lifted him on to the chair next to her, and went back to her dinner.

But, once he was sitting comfortably, the frog spoke again.

"Please, Princess, push your plate closer to me so that I can eat from it," he said. So the princess pushed her plate towards the frog. She was not at all pleased about sharing her dinner with a stinky, slimy spring frog, and she tried her best to pretend he wasn't there.

But, once he had eaten his full, the frog spoke again.

"Please, Princess, carry me upstairs and put me on your pillow so I may sleep." At this point the princess went a rather deep shade of pink – for who in the world would want a sticky, squelchy frog sleeping on their pillow? But alas, she was bound by her promise, so she took the frog up to her bedroom and placed him on her bed. As soon as the frog's head touched the soft and springy pillow, he fell fast asleep.

The following morning, as the sun rose in the sky, the frog left the castle and returned to the woods. When the princess awoke he was gone.

What a relief! she thought, enormously happy that he was no longer there. *I hope I never see that unpleasant little frog ever again.*

But alas, that would not be the case, for when the princess sat down to dinner that evening, she heard the frog calling for her again. As before, the frog ate from her plate and slept in her bed – and it was not just that night, but the next night, too. For *three nights in a row* the frog stayed with the princess, and the princess unhappily endured it. Each morning, the frog would leave before the princess woke up – each morning, that is, except the third.

On the third morning when the princess awoke, someone *was* in her room, but it was *not* the frog.

It was a *prince*!

The princess was somewhat taken aback by the prince's presence – where had he come from and *what*, she asked, was he doing in her bedroom? The prince told her how he had been turned into a frog by a spiteful fairy who had cast a powerful enchantment on him. The only way it could be broken was if a princess invited him into her castle, and let him eat from her plate and sleep on her pillow *for three nights*. Well, as you know, the princess had done all of those things, even though at the time she had not been at all happy about it. To thank her, the prince wished to take the princess to his father's kingdom so that she could be celebrated as a hero at his homecoming.

It did not take long for the princess to agree, and as soon as she did a beautiful carriage pulled up outside the castle to take them home. Behind the carriage rode Heinrich, the prince's most dear and faithful companion. Even though almost everyone had believed the prince dead, Heinrich had travelled far and wide to find him and on seeing the prince once more his heart almost burst with happiness.

Rapunzel

It is thought that the earliest known version of "Rapunzel" was "Petrosinella" by Italian author Giambattista Basile. This version predated both Charlotte-Rose de Caumont de La Force's "Persinette" that was published in France 1698 and also Friedrich Schulz's "Rapunzel" that published in Germany in 1790. However, it was the Grimm version that really found popularity when it published in 1812. "Rapunzel" also became part of Scottish author Andrew Lang's *The Red Fairy Book* collection in 1890.

Once upon a time, a woman lived with her dear husband. Their home was modest but happy, and they did not wish for much in life for they were blessed with each other. Next to them lived a mysterious woman to whom they had never spoken. Her garden was protected by a very tall brick wall, and the husband and wife never saw anyone go in or out of it. And yet it was beautiful – filled with the most fragrant flowers and beautiful blooms that could be smelled all the way over the wall.

It just so happened that, one summer, the husband and wife found out that they were going to have a baby. They celebrated this and were eager for the child's arrival. During the months that followed, the wife started to bloom just as the flowers in their garden had. Their beloved child was growing within her stomach, and this made the husband and wife very happy.

One morning, while the wife was leaning out of her upstairs window, she caught sight of a plant called rapunzel that was growing in the garden next to theirs. On seeing it, a strange craving possessed the woman. So strong was her desire to taste the plant that she found herself unable to consume anything else. "Dear wife, please eat something," said her husband with worry. But though she tried, no food would pass her lips. It was as if she were bewitched.

Every day the wife spoke of the lush rapunzel that grew on the other side of the wall. "If I could only eat some," she said, "my craving would be satisfied." But her husband was fearful. "We have never spoken to the woman who lives there, but still we have always feared her. What would happen to us if we stole from her?" The wife knew this to be true, but was so unable to control the craving that now overtook her. Not able to eat a morsel, she became terribly sick – so sick that soon her husband knew that they had no choice but to procure some forbidden rapunzel from the garden next door.

In the dark of the night he scaled the wall, deftly climbing over and landing on the other side with hardly a noise. Silently he cut leaves from the rapunzel plant and tucked them into his pocket. On his return, he made a salad for his wife and presented it to her cautiously, worried that she still wouldn't eat. But eat she did! With every bite, the wife felt her strength return, and her husband breathed a sigh of relief. They went to sleep that night thinking that their worries were over; so it was with great disappointment that when they awoke the wife was once again overcome with her craving for rapunzel. Once again, no other food would do. Because of this, her husband visited the garden many times over a number of weeks, always at night, always by sneaking over the wall and silently stealing the rapunzel away. For a while, they were able to be happy, as the wife contentedly ate the rapunzel her husband brought her each night. But this was not to last. One night, as the husband climbed the tall wall and landed quietly on the other side, he found himself face to face with the mysterious woman who lived there. In that moment, he realized that the woman was a witch.

"What right have you to steal what is mine?" she asked the man fiercely. He tried to explain, to say that his wife would die without the rapunzel, but the woman would not be calmed. Until, that is, he mentioned their unborn child. Upon hearing this, the witch gave pause. "A child…?" she whispered, almost to herself. "Then you may take as much rapunzel as you wish…" The man cried out with thanks, and such was his joy that tears sprung from his eyes. But he had spoken too soon, and the woman told him so. "You may take the rapunzel," she said again, "but as you have taken from me, so shall I take from you. When your child is born, she will belong to me."

The man heard her words with horror and tried to argue with her, but it was no good. The decision was made. And so the man made his way back over the wall that night with sadness in his heart. He made the decision not to tell his wife what had happened, for it would make her terribly unhappy. So for a few months the wife felt contentment, knowing that her child was growing larger and stronger inside of her, and not knowing the awful price they would have to pay once their child was born.

On the day of their baby's birth, the sun shone brightly and it was as if every plant and every flower had opened to welcome the child into the world. It was with enormous joy that the husband and wife saw their child was a girl. But their joy was short lived. No sooner was the baby girl placed in her mother's arms, than the witch appeared. "It is time for you to pay your debt to me," she said. The wife was momentarily confused, but when she saw her husband collapse with grief she understood what had transpired and wept as the witch took her child away. As she carried the baby back through her garden, the witch decided that the stolen plant would become the child's namesake: she would call her Rapunzel.

To prevent her parents finding her, the witch stole away with Rapunzel in the darkness of night, taking her to a secluded tower that soared high above the trees. No one would find them there, but if they did they would never be able to enter the tower, for it had no door and only one window, which was found near the very top. The witch forced Rapunzel to stay inside, never allowing her to leave, and made her grow her hair long so that the witch herself could use it to come and go from the dwelling. Every evening at sundown, the witch would climb down Rapunzel's hair and disappear into the darkness of the forest, leaving Rapunzel alone in her prison. But despite all of this, Rapunzel grew into a clever and determined young woman over the years, reading the witch's many books while she was away from the castle each night and forming her own opinions about the world that lay outside of the tower. When the witch returned, she would call up to Rapunzel, shouting,

"Rapunzel!

Rapunzel!

Throw down your hair."

Rapunzel would rush to put the books back in place before standing before the window and throwing her hair down to the witch.

This is how life continued for Rapunzel and the witch for many years, and nothing changed. Nothing, that is, until one night when a prince rode by on his way back to his kingdom. As his horse cantered through the trees, the prince became aware of someone singing. So lonely did the voice sound, it haunted him. He followed the sound until he found the tower, which, despite its height, he had never before spotted. *Could it be enchanted?* he wondered, and he decided to hide near it awhile in case of any dangers. There he sat for hours, until the sun started rising far away on the horizon. The prince was just about to emerge from his hiding place when he saw a woman approach in a dark cape with a hood. He watched her from a distance.

"Rapunzel!

Rapunzel!

Throw down your hair," he heard the woman shout, and in a moment he saw a large tumble of hair travel from the window above and reach all the way to the ground. *A rope made of hair!* he thought to himself. *What witchcraft is this? And what lies in that tower?* He resolved to wait for the witch to leave so that he could investigate for himself. It wasn't until nightfall that the prince's patience was rewarded by the soft *thud* of hair hitting the ground: the witch was leaving the tower. The prince stayed in hiding as the witch climbed down, and waited a while longer to make sure she was not going to come straight back. When at last he felt confident that the coast was clear, the prince went over to the foot of the tower.

"Rapunzel!

Rapunzel!

Throw down your hair," he whispered, as loud as he dared. There was a pause, and for a moment the prince wondered if it had worked. But, just as he was about to walk away, he saw hair lowering from the window above. As it touched the ground, the prince reached out for it and was surprised by its softness. *How can something so soft be so strong?* he wondered as he made his way up. Upon reaching the top, he was shocked to hear a girl's voice asking, "Why is it you are back so soon?" He pulled himself over the window ledge and, before he knew it, stood face to face with Rapunzel.

With alarm, he listened as Rapunzel told him of her life imprisoned in the tower. "But now that I have been found," she said, "I may be able to escape." The prince promised to help her in any way that he could. He questioned Rapunzel on the tower – was there another way out, besides the window? But with sadness Rapunzel replied that there was not. After all, she had been trying to escape for many, many years. But then a thought occurred to her: if the prince brought her enough silk to fashion a ladder, she would be able to climb down that and be free. The prince promised at once and agreed to return for as many nights as it would take for them to sew the silk into a ladder.

In the nights that followed, the prince did as he had said and brought as much silk as he could come by.

"Rapunzel!

Rapunzel!

Throw down your hair," he would call each time. As he and Rapunzel sat side by side to sew the ladder together, they would talk of the books they had read. Soon enough a friendship started to grow. But one night, when the prince was still making his way through the forest to Rapunzel, the witch returned early. "With the silk you have brought me, my escape will surely come soon," called out Rapunzel, mistakenly thinking that it was the prince who was climbing through the window. At this, the witch flew into a terrible rage. Unlocking a wooden chest, she retrieved a pair of scissors and pinned Rapunzel down, cutting at her hair until it was jagged and short. With her magic, the witch took Rapunzel deep into the wilderness of the forest and left her there to fend for herself.

When she returned to the tower, the witch tied Rapunzel's hair to the window and lay in wait for the prince. It was not long before she heard him call,

"Rapunzel!

Rapunzel!

Throw down your hair," and she threw Rapunzel's shorn hair over the threshold and down to the unsuspecting prince, who started to climb up at once. Up and up climbed the prince, not knowing who it was that he was climbing towards, until he reached the top, where the witch was waiting. When the witch revealed herself to him he recoiled in horror, and such was his shock that he lost hold of the hair to which he was clinging. With a loud and desperate shriek, he fell to the ground and landed in a thorn bush. As he tried to get out, the thorns scratched at his eyes, making it difficult for him to see, and in pain he stumbled into the forest.

For days and nights he wandered, not really knowing where he was for his eyes were terribly damaged. Until one day when he heard a familiar sound: the most sweet and haunting song that he remembered as if he had heard it just yesterday. He stumbled towards the sound, hoping that it would never stop, hoping that the singer would continue for as long as it took him to find them, and with every step the prince knew that the voice was getting louder. But then it stopped abruptly. The prince sank to his knees in desperation, for without the voice to follow, how would he find the singer? But then he felt a hand upon his face. It was Rapunzel; she had run to him. As they hugged each other with happiness, Rapunzel's tears of joy ran into the prince's eyes and helped them heal. As he blinked back his own tears, he looked at Rapunzel and smiled. They were both safe at last.

The Elves and the Shoemaker

When Grimm's *Children's and Household Tales* published in Germany in 1812, it contained three stories under the group title of "Die Wichtelmänner" (later translated to "The Elves"). "The Elves and the Shoemaker" was the first of those tales.

There was once a husband and wife who were shoemakers. Unfortunately, though they worked very hard, and were honest and good people, over time they became extremely poor. So poor, in fact, that they barely had enough money to live. They sold all of their belongings so that they had money for food, but soon enough there was no more to sell, and all that remained for them was a small amount of leather – just enough to make one pair of shoes.

That evening, they sat down in their workshop and cut the leather to size. Tomorrow, they decided, would be the day that they would make their last pair of shoes. The shoemakers hoped the shoes would sell – and for a decent price – so that they could buy food.

Before they went to sleep, the shoemakers laid out the leather carefully. They would start work as soon as the sun rose the next day, they decided. Filled with determination and hope, the husband and wife slept soundly that night.

The following morning, the husband woke early and went straight to the workshop. But to his surprise, where the pieces of leather had once lain, the shoemaker now saw a pair of the most beautiful shoes. His surprise turned to wonder as he picked them up and studied them – the stitching was so small and neat. Such craftsmanship! The shoemaker had never seen a pair of shoes so beautifully made. But where had they come from? That day, a customer came to the shoemaker and was so enamoured by the shoes that they insisted on paying a very high price for them. The shoemakers were amazed. Not only did they now have enough money for food, but they could also buy enough leather to make two new pairs of shoes! That evening, as before, they cut the leather to size and laid it out carefully in the workshop, going to bed early so that they could wake with the birds and start work on the two pairs of shoes.

But when the wife walked into their workshop the next morning, there was no work to be done, for there, right in front of her were *two* pairs of extraordinary shoes! She picked up both pairs and studied them with admiration – they really were faultless. It did not take long for both pairs of shoes to be sold, and – again – for a very good price. So the shoemakers bought even *more* leather – this time enough for four pairs of shoes – and did the same as they had done the previous two nights. And I'm sure you can guess what the shoemakers saw the next morning? That's right! Four pairs of exquisitely made shoes!

And so it went on for some time, with the leather always turning into pairs of shoes overnight. The shoemakers marvelled at their good fortune – how lucky they were! The remarkable shoes had helped them to thrive again – not only had they become the most well known shoemakers in the land, but people travelled far and wide to buy shoes from them.

But who was helping them? As the husband and wife chatted one evening, they decided they would like to find out. When night fell, they prepared the leather for the following morning just as they always had. But instead of going to bed, they left a candle burning and hid behind a curtain hung in a corner of the workshop. As the hours passed and the night grew darker, they watched and waited. And as the clock struck midnight, they saw something that took their breath away. There, in the workshop, appeared two tiny elves. They sat at the shoemaker's bench and quickly set to work arranging the leather and sewing it in place. The most surprising thing of all was that the two elves were not wearing a stitch of clothing. Not a thing! The shoemakers could not quite believe their eyes. They watched the elves in astonishment as they worked silently and skilfully. And when the elves were finished, they disappeared just as quickly as they had appeared in the first place.

Well! The shoemakers were quite stunned, and they went to bed without so much as a word to each other, such was their amazement. In the morning, when they found themselves able to speak again, they discussed the elves and their handsome handiwork.

"But why do they not have clothes?" asked the wife. And the husband had to admit that he did not know. It made them both feel worried for the elves. It would soon be winter, and what would happen then? The elves could freeze without even so much as a coat for their backs. And so it was decided: as the elves had brought such enormous good fortune to the shoemakers, they would make the elves some clothes to say thank you.

They set to work immediately, sewing two small shirts, two waistcoats and two coats, as well as two pairs of trousers. Lastly, they made two very small pairs of extremely fine shoes. Making the clothes for the elves made the shoemaker and his wife feel immensely happy, and they smiled that evening as they stood in the workshop – for instead of laying out leather for shoes, they laid out the newly made clothes for the elves. As midnight neared, they hid again behind the curtain and wondered what the elves would do upon seeing their gifts. They didn't need to wonder for long, because no sooner had they hidden than the elves appeared and made their way quickly to the workbench where they expected to see the leather laid out for them. But when they saw the clothes they laughed with delight, and picked up each item to look at it closely. Quickly, they got dressed – and laughed even more, for they were so unused to seeing each other in clothes that the sight alone made them very happy indeed! They jumped and danced all the way out of the workshop.

That was the last time the shoemakers were visited by the elves, but they thought of them often throughout their long and happy lives, and were forever grateful for their generosity.

The Little Mermaid

"The Little Mermaid", or *"Den Lille Havfrue"* as it is known in Danish, was written by Hans Christian Andersen. Published in Denmark in 1837, as part of *Fairy Tales Told For Children*, it has inspired many retellings – both in book and film.

Many years ago, in the depths of the deepest ocean, much further than any human has ever travelled, stood the underwater kingdom of the Sea King. With walls of coral and a roof made of glistening shells, the Sea King's palace stood in the centre of the kingdom and was the most beautiful place in all the world.

There the Sea King lived with his six daughters and their grandmother, who had looked after the girls ever since the Sea King had become a widow. To show that she was a woman of high standing, the grandmother wore twelve sparkling pearls in her tail, while other mer-people of importance would wear only six.

The six princesses were all very beautiful – the youngest in particular, her eyes as deep in colour as the sea in which they lived.

The princesses knew that on the nights of their fifteenth birthdays they would each be allowed to rise to the surface and be above the water for the first time. The youngest princess was a quiet and thoughtful child, and she dreamt of her journey to the surface even more than her sisters did, despite the fact that she had to wait the longest. As her sisters came of age and ascended to the distant light above she watched them with curiosity and an aching heart, and every day she would ask her grandmother questions about the other world.

What do their legs look like? she would say.

How do they adorn themselves? Why can we not show ourselves to them? And each time, her grandmother would give a patient reply.

Their legs are unusual – like nothing you've ever seen before, she would answer.

They adorn themselves with clothes, made from materials unknown to us. We must never willingly reveal our existence to them, for they will fear us and be repulsed by us.

The little mermaid listened to all of this in wonder, and continued to dream of her fifteenth birthday when she would finally be able to rise to the surface. As each year passed, she watched her sisters with longing as their birthdays came and went. Each sister would come back from the surface with a new story, or an object they had found – although they all knew that the best finds appeared after a storm, when the boats had been thrown about and perhaps even turned into wreckages, resting, full of treasures, on the seabed. After one particularly terrible storm, the little mermaid came across a large statue of a boy who looked to be the same age as her. How beautiful he was, and how sad his eyes were. She visited the statue every day, feeling at peace to be near it.

When at last the little mermaid's fifteenth birthday arrived, her grandmother placed a wreath of white lilies upon her hair and weaved eight bright pearls into her tail. The little mermaid's pain was sharp as her grandmother did this. "You are now grown up," said her grandmother, with sadness in her eyes, "And there are times at which we must suffer pain."

As the little mermaid made her way up to the surface, she felt as light as a bubble rising through the water. The sun, bleeding orange and pink in the sky, had almost set as she raised her head above the waves and breathed air for the very first time. At once she was struck by the beauty of this world, so new and unknown to her. With surprise, and not a little bit of fear, she saw that a large ship was sailing nearby, its three white sails standing proud in the night sky. There was music and singing aboard the ship, and the little mermaid just couldn't help herself; bursting with curiosity, she swam over and carefully watched the people on board through the cabin windows. She meant to stay only a moment, but seconds stretched to minutes and minutes stretched to hours, and she did not notice as darkness fell around her, so bewitched was she by the humans. There was one in particular from whom she could not pull her eyes away – a young man with dark hair and dark eyes, whose skin shone in the moonlight. After some time she realized he was a prince whose birthday was being celebrated by all upon the ship. *Many happy returns, Your Royal Highness!* the people cried with much merriment, and they set rockets shooting into the darkness of the night sky, making it as bright as day. The little mermaid was so startled that she dived beneath the waves, but she quickly returned and saw hundreds of stars falling all around her. Such magical fireworks she had never before seen.

It became very late, and the little mermaid watched until the humans became quiet and the lights went out. No more rockets shot into the sky. But as she turned to leave, the little mermaid saw the dark clouds on the horizon, and felt the power in the waves. There was a storm coming. And it came quickly, making the ship groan under the weight of the water throwing it this way and that. The humans called out in fear as lightning flashed across the skies above them and water fell so heavily it was as if the sea was both above and below. The little mermaid looked for the prince, and for a moment everything went black, but thunder clapped, and with it lightning set the world alight. She searched for the prince and saw him just as he fell into the ocean.

No! she thought. *He must not die!*

Her strong tail put her by the prince's side within a moment and she grasped him tightly, keeping his head above the water. Looking about her desperately, she swam towards the land she spied in the distance, struggling with the prince but nonetheless managing to keep him alive. She was certain that he would have died had she not been there.

When she finally reached land, the sun was starting to rise, and with it a golden light stretched across the sea. *So calm it looks now*, she thought. *So peaceful. I would not believe the destruction it could cause had I not seen it with my own eyes.*

The little mermaid brought the prince as far on to the land as she was able, pulling him through the fine white sand that shone in the sunlight, and quickly swimming back into the water to lie in wait behind a large rock that stood high. It was not long before a girl appeared and, upon seeing the prince, the girl let out a gasp. She ran to him, and placed her hand upon his face as she called for help. As the little mermaid looked on, the prince opened his eyes. He was alive! He smiled at the people standing around him, and though this should have made the little mermaid happy, instead it made her sad – for the prince did not smile upon her.

Back in her underwater world, the little mermaid became even more quiet and thoughtful than she had been before. It seemed that she never stopped thinking of the world above, and never stopped dreaming of the prince. It was making her deeply unhappy, and her family worried for her, but no matter what they did they could not change the way she felt.

The little mermaid became so desperate that she made a terrible choice: one night, when she knew her sisters to be asleep, she swam out of the palace and through the kingdom that was silent in sleep. Further she travelled, and the beautiful plant life turned to grey marshes as she travelled further and further still before coming to the whirlpools behind which a terrible sorceress lived. She had never been to this place before, and fear gripped her heart like nothing she had ever known, but so compelled was she that she continued. It was here that she found the lair of the sea witch, whose abode stood dark and looming, built with the bones of humans long lost to the sea, and surrounded by dark, thick branches that swayed like arms beneath the water. The little mermaid very nearly turned back, so scared was she, but she remembered the prince and her courage returned. And as she approached the entranceway, the little mermaid saw the sea witch sitting upon a throne of sorts, surrounded by water snakes.

"I know what you seek," said the sea witch, and it was as if her voice was everywhere all at once. "If you give up your tail, you will never get it back. Is that really what you wish?"

"Yes," replied the little mermaid, and she meant it. The sea witch sighed. "I can give you legs, but they will come at a price. What you desire requires great magic." The little mermaid listened in horror. "There exists a potion that will take away your tail and leave legs where it once was. If you can make the prince fall in love with you, then you shall become a human just like him. But know this," she continued, and she looked at the little mermaid with deep concern. "Every step will bring you pain, every time your feet touch the ground it will feel as if you are walking on knives; as long as you walk you will suffer. And if you fail to make the prince fall in love with you, you can never return to your life as a mermaid. You will perish. You will no longer live'."

The little mermaid's hand flew to her mouth, such was her shock, and yet the sea witch continued. "That is not all," she said, fixing her bright blue eyes upon the mermaid in front of her. "If you *truly* want this, you must pay the ultimate price. You must give me your voice."

At this the little mermaid gave pause. "But if you take my voice, then what is left of me?" she asked. The sea witch shrugged. "If you will bear all of this, I will help you," she said, simply.

The little mermaid could only nod – so great was her fear that it was as if she had already lost her voice – and the sea witch nodded in return as she held out her hand. A small vial appeared within it, containing a liquid darker than the deepest depths of the ocean. "It is done," said the sea witch, as the little mermaid took the vial and swam away. "It is done."

The little mermaid swam quickly away from the house made of bones and the branches that seemed to grab at her as she passed. She saw the palace in the distance. *Should I return to say goodbye?* she wondered. But the coward within her said no. Up, up, up she swam, up to the surface, up to the light. And as she broke through the water, for a moment she felt happiness at what she had done. She swam to the water's edge, where the sea met the land, and carefully unclasped the tip of the vial. Drinking the liquid inside, she felt a strange sensation travel across her tail, separating her from the life she once knew. The pain was so great that she fell unconscious.

After some time, the little mermaid started to come to, and realized that someone stood before her. It was the prince! "Who are you?" he asked. "Where have you come from?" And she tried to talk, but no words would leave her lips. Looking down, she saw that her tail was gone, and in its place were two human legs. With no clothes, she could only wrap herself in her long, thick hair, and as she stood pain shot through her legs and to the soles of her feet. She was reminded of the sea witch's warning.

Oh how quickly she had agreed to this suffering! But she looked at the prince, saw him looking at her with concern, and pushed the worry from her mind. With every step bringing tears to her eyes, the little mermaid walked to the palace with the prince.

Upon her arrival she was taken to a room of her own and given clothes to wear, and she marvelled at how beautiful she looked – for she was indeed beautiful. She had been the loveliest of all her sisters and now here, upon land, she found that she was even lovelier still. But the loss of her voice haunted her.

The prince decided that she should stay with him always. She slept at the foot of his bed and accompanied him everywhere on horseback. But at night, when everyone in the palace had fallen asleep, the little mermaid would sit on the large marble steps of the palace and bathe her burning feet in the cold and salty seawater that rushed nearby. One night she spotted her sisters in the distance, their arms linked and their eyes searching. They sang sorrowfully for their lost sister.

As days passed, the little mermaid grew more in love with the prince, but feared that he did not feel the same way. Though he treated her well and was indeed kind, he did not seem to love her, and one day the prince was instructed by his mother to visit the princess who lived in the next kingdom, for it was she who he was betrothed to marry. At first the prince resisted, but he finally relented and set off on his journey, leaving the little mermaid behind. It seemed as though the prince was gone for days, and all the while the little mermaid felt her time running out. *What will it feel like to cease to exist?* she wondered. *To become the foam of the sea, a part of nature.* But she resolved not to give up hope. It wasn't until the prince returned with his bride to be that the little mermaid's heart truly broke. It was the girl who had found him on the beach, after the little mermaid had rescued him. He believed the girl to be the reason he was still alive, and he loved her so because of it. Turning to the little mermaid, he smiled. "Now that I have found my love, my dreams are fulfilled," he told her. "I know you will rejoice for me, as your devotion is complete and sincere." The little mermaid kissed his hand and turned away as a tear rolled down her cheek. In that moment it felt as if her heart were truly breaking.

It was decreed that the prince's wedding would take place the following day. As the kingdom prepared for the joyous occasion, the little mermaid prepared for her end. On the morrow, church bells rang and people cheered. The little mermaid, dressed in silk and gold, held up the train of the bride's wedding dress as she walked down the aisle and could say nothing to anyone. The celebrations went on into the evening, with the prince and his wife welcoming their guests on to a lavish boat. Cannons fired, flags were waved and lamps were lit. All about the little mermaid people celebrated, but no one stopped to pay attention to the beautiful girl with sadness in her eyes who could not speak. This was the last night she would breathe the air of this world, the little mermaid knew, and as the music played she felt something stirring in her heart – the spirit of the girl she used to be, perhaps – and she started to dance. The people watched in wonder, such was the beauty of her movement. She glided through the air, not thinking about the needles that seemed to press into her feet and the ache that she felt now more than ever upon her legs. As the music grew faint and the little mermaid stopped dancing, the crowd that surrounded her cheered loudly, but as she looked for the prince he was nowhere to be seen.

Walking on to the deck of the ship at midnight, the little mermaid looked out across the sea and saw the silhouettes of her sisters swimming towards her. As they neared, she saw that their hair, once long, was now gone. Their beautiful faces looked up at her from below.

"We gave our hair to the sea witch so that we might help you," they said, and they presented her with a knife. "If you plunge this into the heart of the prince before the sun rises, you will be free to return to your life beneath the sea. Please, dear sister, please return to us." The little mermaid took the knife in her hand and walked to find the prince.

On finding him sleeping peacefully, the little mermaid brushed the hair from his face as the prince sighed the name of his bride in his sleep. *How foolish I have been*, she thought, as the knife trembled in her hand. But she could not do it. She could not! Returning to the deck of the ship, the little mermaid looked up at the morning sky now soaked in the most heavenly light. Lowering herself into the water, she at last felt relief from the pain of her legs and the burden of her mistake. As the seawater overcame her body, she released one last breath as she dissolved to foam within the waves.

The Turnip

Featured in volume two of the Brothers Grimm's *Children's and Household Tales*, "The Turnip" is thought to be the result of two tales – "The Gigantic Turnip" and "Two Presents to the King" – being merged into one at some point in history.

Once there were two brothers who were both soldiers, but that was where the similarities ended for them, as, amongst many other things, one was rich and one was poor. The poor brother wanted to build a better life for himself so, abandoning his life as a soldier, he decided to become a gardener and live off the crops he grew on his small piece of land. Every day he tended the soil with care, digging the earth and sowing seeds.

Before long, green shoots started to appear: his crops were beginning to grow. Looking over his garden, the poor brother felt proud.

As his garden flourished, the brother noticed that one vegetable was growing far bigger than the rest: a turnip. Each day it swelled larger and larger – in fact, it seemed as though it would never stop! But stop it finally did, and on that day the poor brother stared at it in wonder. It was a truly marvellous turnip – certainly the biggest he had ever seen! But what could he do with such a thing? No one would want to buy this enormous vegetable, for surely it would rot before they could eat it all? Besides, the sweetest turnips were the small ones, not the big ones.

Perhaps, thought the brother, *I should present my turnip to the king, as a gift. That may be the best use for such an oversized vegetable.*

So he yoked his oxen, hauled the turnip on to his cart and made his way to the king's castle. Once there, he presented it proudly.

"What a *tremendous* turnip!" said the king – for he had seen many things in his life, but never before had he seen such a large turnip. The sight made him extremely curious, and he proceeded to ask the gardener a number of questions.

"Where did you get the seed?" he asked. "And how did you become so lucky? Why, you must truly be a man of good fortune!"

But the poor brother was quick in his honesty, and replied,

"In truth, your majesty, I am no man of good fortune. I am poor, and was once a soldier but am now a gardener. I tend to my land so I can live. I have a brother who is very rich and all the world knows him for his richness. But because I am poor, nobody knows of me."

The king took pity on him then, saying, "Dear

man, you shall be poor no longer. I will give you so much that you shall be richer than even your brother."

The king bestowed upon the gardener gold, fine clothes, flocks of livestock and even land, and made him so rich that his belongings dwarfed those of his brother by far.

News of the man who had become rich because of a turnip quickly travelled across the land, and it wasn't long before the gardener's brother himself heard it. Upon doing so, he immediately became envious and fell into a rage. *How could someone as lowly as my poor brother come into such good fortune?* he wondered. The rich brother thought himself to be superior to the poor brother in many ways, including intellect, and he started to plan how he could trick the king into giving him riches greater than the ones given to his brother. *If my brother received gold and land when all he gave the king was a turnip,* he thought, *then I must give the king a very grand gift indeed, for then he will reward me with treasures that are even grander still.*

He prepared the most lavish collection of gold and jewels to bestow upon the king, and after travelling to the castle he presented the trove proudly. The king accepted his gift graciously, but also with much contemplation, as he wondered what he could possibly give the rich man who stood before him in return. After all, what do you give someone who already has everything they need and more? After much thought, an idea struck him: as the rich brother already had gold and jewels and land, the king would give him the turnip! The rich brother had no choice but to accept the turnip as his gift, as he couldn't refuse the king. He even had to drag it home with him – and for this he was deeply annoyed.

Once home, the rich brother was filled with anger and wicked thoughts. He cursed his once-poor brother and blamed him for the loss of his own riches and the gain of this silly oversized turnip. As revenge, he resolved to kill his brother.

He hired some villains to do the deed and, once he had shown them where to lie in wait, he went in deception to speak with his brother.

"Dear brother," he said, "I have found buried treasure! Come – join me in digging for it, and we shall share the riches between us."

Well, the once-poor brother had no reason to think that he was being told anything but the truth, so he readily agreed. But as the two brothers were travelling along the dusty road at dusk, the villains set upon the once-poor brother. They bound him up, intending to hang him on a tree. But before they could do so they were startled by the sound of horse hooves in the distance. Not knowing who was approaching, they quickly pushed the brother into a sack head first, and hung the sack from the tree before fleeing like cowards.

While he was up there, the once-poor brother worked away at the sack and was able to make a hole large enough to poke his head through. When a horseman appeared, the brother saw that the traveller was in fact a young student journeying on his nag, and singing as he went. As the man went to pass beneath the tree, the brother called out to him.

"Good day, my dear fellow!"

The student looked this way and that, but for the life of him he could not see where the voice was coming from.

"Who calls to me?" he replied. To which the brother answered, "Look upwards!" Continuing, he said, "Here I lie in the sack of wisdom. It is here that I, in but a short time, have learned many great and wondrous things. By staying here a while longer, I will learn all that humankind can know and shall come forth wiser than the wisest person. Oh, that anyone could but feel the power of such knowledge."

The student listened to all of this with great interest, and pondered awhile. At last he said, "Blessed be the day and hour when I found you, for our encounter is most fortunate indeed. Pray, cannot you let me into the sack for a little while?"

The brother did his best to hide his smile from the student while he pretended to dwell on the question.

"Hmm," he replied slowly. "I *may* allow you to spend some time in this extraordinary sack, but you must first wait patiently so that I may stay here but another hour to learn some of what is still unknown to me."

The student agreed, and made himself comfortable on the ground beside the tree. But time weighed heavily upon him and before long he begged to ascend the tree immediately. The brother pretended to oblige, saying, "Oh, very well then," and instructed the student to untie the rope and lower him to the ground.

Once the student had done as much, and untied the sack to set the brother free, he cried out in excitement, saying,

"Now! Let me ascend quickly!" and he began to get into the sack feet first.

"One moment," said the brother, "for that is the wrong way. You must go in with your head first..."

He pushed the student in, tied up the sack and swung him up on to the very branch he himself had swung from but moments before.

"How is it up there?" he asked, as the student dangled in the air. "Do you feel the wisdom flowing into you? Now, rest there in peace until you are a wiser man than you once were."

And with that, he trotted off on the young boy's nag and left the silly fellow to hang in the sack until someone came by to help him down.

Cinderella

Also known as "The Little Glass Slipper", the story of Cinderella is thought to have derived from the Greek story of "Rhodopis", which originated in around 7 BC. The first European version was Giambattista Basile's "Pentamerone", which published in 1634, however Charles Perrault and the Brothers Grimm versions are the most popular, with the former publishing in *Histories ou Contes du Temps Passé* in 1697 and the latter publishing in 1812.

There was once a gentleman who, after the death of his first wife, found himself a widower. His daughter, a lovely child of sweet nature, very much took after her mother, and for this and many other reasons her father loved her so.

After some time, the gentleman decided to remarry and chose a woman who had also experienced tragedy, as she was a widow herself. The woman had two daughters from her previous marriage, and the gentleman felt himself very fortunate to have met such a wonderful woman as she, for she appeared kind and genial.

But looks can be deceiving. No sooner had the wedding taken place, than the stepmother and stepsisters revealed their true natures – but not to the gentleman, only to his daughter. The stepmother could not bear to see the affection her new husband held for his daughter, as she wanted it all for herself. She encouraged her own daughters to act selfishly and spitefully towards the girl, and because of this they gave her coarse clothes and made her do the hardest of work around the house. She brushed and mopped the floors, scoured the dishes, dusted the cobwebs, cleaned her stepmother's and stepsisters' chambers … and this she did every day. While the rest of the family slept in fine rooms with comfortable beds, the gentleman's daughter slept on a straw bed nestled next to the chimney amongst the cinders and ashes. Her stepmother and stepsisters soon started calling her Cinderella.

When Cinderella tried to tell her father about everything she endured, he turned her away, for his love for Cinderella's stepmother had made him blind to the truth. And so, she found herself in the sorriest of states. But she bore it all determinedly, unwilling to let the behaviour of others break her spirit.

One day, Cinderella's stepsisters rushed into the drawing room in much excitement, speaking of a royal ball that was to take place. The entire kingdom was invited, and the girls immediately started planning outfits and discussing hairstyles. Indeed, they talked all day long of nothing but what they might wear to the ball. But while Cinderella knew that every person in the kingdom was invited, she also knew that she could not go to the ball. After all, what would she wear? Her coarse clothes were not right for the occasion and her stepsisters would not allow her to borrow any of their dresses.

On the night of the ball, Cinderella helped her stepmother and stepsisters make the finishing touches to their dresses. As her family rushed to their awaiting carriage in excitement, Cinderella stood at the door unable to pass over the threshold. There she stayed until the carriage was but a dot on the horizon, and when she felt sure that no one would see, Cinderella started to cry.

"My dear, why do you cry so?" came a voice from nearby. Looking up, Cinderella saw the kindest of fairies standing before her. With rosy cheeks and a dress that shone like stars in the night sky, the fairy godmother was the most enchanting creature Cinderella had ever set eyes upon. "I had wished to go to the ball," said Cinderella through her tears, "but I know that the palace is no place for me."

Her fairy godmother leaned close and lifted Cinderella's head high. "My dear, your place in this world is wherever you believe it to be," she said, "and if you wish to go to the ball, then go to the ball you must!" With that, the fairy godmother lifted her wand and let it glide through the air. The magic glistened and sparkled around them as a pumpkin flew from its place in the garden and turned into a fine gold carriage before Cinderella's own eyes. Six mice became six fine black horses, and a large rat was turned into a cheery coachman. Finally, six lizards from the well were turned into the smartest footmen Cinderella had ever seen.

"You see?" said her fairy godmother. "Wishes can come true."

Cinderella made to get into the carriage, for, in her amazement, she had quite forgotten the rags that she was wearing. But her fairy godmother called out her name. As Cinderella spun around, the fairy touched her wand to Cinderella, and a glittering light enveloped her. When the light had faded, there stood Cinderella in the most beautiful dress of gold and silver, beset with the purest of jewels. Upon her feet were slippers made of glass. Cinderella gasped as she looked down upon them.

"Now hurry, Cinderella, hurry!" called the fairy, as Cinderella got into the carriage. "But remember this: on the stroke of midnight, all that has been transformed will once again return to what it was. You must come home before midnight!"

"I will, dear fairy godmother, I will!" said Cinderella in return, and off she went to the ball.

When Cinderella entered the grand hall, a rush ran throughout the crowd.

"Who is that?" someone asked.

"Where has she come from?"

The prince, who up until that moment had been quite disinterested in dancing or speaking to anyone, rushed to be the first to dance with the beautiful new guest. He enjoyed Cinderella's company so much that he did his best to stay by her side throughout the whole evening, even during the meal when he forgot to eat because he was gazing so intently at her. Cinderella had never experienced such finery, and took moments to appreciate everything she saw, touched and tasted. She tried a little bit of all of the foods, and was delighted by their flavours, and she danced for hours on end with the prince. But Cinderella was enjoying herself so much that she did not realize the time, and it was only when the clock started to chime midnight that she looked up at the prince in panic.

"I have to go!" she cried, and she started to break into a run.

"But where will I find you?" called the prince after her. "You haven't even told me your name!" Without another word, Cinderella rushed through the palace entrance and down the long stone steps that stood before it. In her haste, one of her glass slippers fell from her feet, and though she didn't want to leave it behind she knew that she could not turn back. As she ran back to her carriage, the royal clock chimed its last chime and the carriage turned back into a pumpkin. Cinderella walked home that night, but it didn't matter, for her head was now filled with such happiness.

The next day, she listened to her stepsisters as they talked of the ball and the beautiful woman who danced with the prince. "I have never seen a dress like hers before," said one of her sisters enviously. "Just where did she get it?"

Cinderella smiled, for of course she would never tell. However, it was not long before news spread across the land that the prince was looking for the mystery woman. He had found her glass slipper and he asked for every eligible woman to come forth to try it on. As the prince travelled from house to house, many women tried on the slipper, but none of them could make it fit. The prince was terribly disappointed.

At last, the prince and his entourage approached the house where Cinderella lived. Her stepsisters rushed to the door in their finest attire and seated themselves quickly, both eager to make the slipper fit. But try as they might (and they really did try!), the slipper of course would not fit them. "Sire, this is the last house in the kingdom," said the prince's most trusted aide. "There are no others."

"But how can that be?" asked the prince in dismay. At that moment, Cinderella stepped out of the shadows. Wearing rags, and skin dirtied by work, Cinderella still looked as lovely as ever, and the prince recognized her immediately. Taking her hand, he led her to a seat so that she may try on the slipper, and as her stepsisters watched in amazement, the slipper slid straight on to Cinderella's foot. It was a perfect fit. The prince cried with joy, and was even more pleased when Cinderella produced the other glass slipper from the pockets of her dress. As she put the second slipper on to her foot, her fairy godmother appeared and transformed Cinderella's clothes, making them finer and even more magnificent than any she had worn before. In an instant, her stepsisters saw that Cinderella had been the woman at the ball, and they cursed themselves for their foolishness. But, as she was so kind-hearted, Cinderella chose to forgive her stepmother and stepsisters for their ugly behaviour, and even her father for his absence and for turning a blind eye. And with that, Cinderella left with the prince, and did not look back.

The Golden Goose

While "The Golden Goose" first appeared in volume one of the Grimm's 1812 fairy tale collection, it has also been retold by other storytellers, including Alexander Afanasyev, who published a collection of Russian folk and fairy tales in eight volumes between 1855 and 1863 and included a tale called "The Princess Who Never Smiled".

Once there lived a man, a woman and their three sons. While the eldest and middle sons were very well liked, the youngest brother was rather quiet and shy, so people often mocked him – for they knew that he would not react.

One bright day, it was decided that the eldest brother would go into the forest to hew a large tree. Cutting trees made for hungry work, so his mother gave him a sweet cake and a bottle of wine to eat and drink after his work was done. When the eldest brother crossed into the forest, he was met by a little grey-haired man. The man bade him good day and said, "May I have a piece of your cake and a drink of your wine? I am so very hungry and thirsty."

The eldest brother did not want to share his food, and he told the man so. "If I give you my cake and wine, I shall have less for myself," he said. "Now be off with you." And the brother left the man standing there alone. But when the eldest brother started to chop at the tree, it was not long before he lost his grip on his axe and cut himself on the arm. He was so terribly injured that he had to go home and have his arm bound up. What the eldest brother didn't realize was that this act was the grey-haired man's doing.

Soon enough, the middle brother went into the forest to fell the tree and, like his brother before him, he too was given cake and wine. As the middle brother crossed the boundary into the forest, the grey-haired man appeared again and asked the brother to share his food and drink. The middle brother also said no and continued on his way, for he wanted to cut down the tree and get home as quickly as he could. However, the middle brother had made but three blows to the tree trunk before he struck himself in the leg. The cut was so severe that he had to be carried home. This act was also the grey-haired man's doing, though still no one realized this.

After seeing his two brothers go to the forest to try to cut down the tree, the youngest brother wanted to do the same.

"Father, please let me go," he said. But his father did not believe he could do it.

"Your brothers tried and they hurt themselves," he said. "You must not meddle in things about which you do not know." Still, the youngest brother persisted, and when his father could take no more he decided to let his son go, telling him, "Perhaps you will grow wiser when you hurt yourself as they did."

Having given all of her good cake and wine to the eldest and middle brothers, the youngest brother's mother gave him a plain cinder cake and a bottle of sour beer to take with him. The younger brother set off happily enough, for he was glad to have been given the chance to prove himself.

When the youngest brother reached the forest, he was met by the little grey-haired man just as his brothers had been, and he too was asked the same question:

"May I have a piece of your cake and a drink of your wine? I am so hungry and thirsty," said the little man.

"I only have cinder cake and sour beer," the youngest brother answered, "but if that pleases you then we will sit down and eat and drink together." The grey-haired man smiled and nodded, and the two sat down. But when the youngest brother unwrapped his cinder cake he saw that it was now a fine sweet cake. And when he swigged the sour beer he discovered that it was now a delicious wine. So they ate and they drank, and once they were done the grey-haired man looked at the youngest brother thoughtfully.

"Since you have a kind heart and have been willing to share the little you have with me, I would like to share something with *you*: go to the old tree yonder and cut it down. Its roots will reveal an object that is very special."

And with that, the little grey-haired man took his leave and the youngest brother was alone in the forest once more. He cut down the tree just as instructed. And when the tree fell hard upon the ground, there in its roots sat a goose with shining feathers of pure gold. The goose let the youngest brother pick it up without complaint. As it had now started to become dark, the youngest brother quickly found an inn where he could stay for the night.

The innkeeper had three daughters, all of whom saw the goose and looked upon its golden feathers with wonder. The eldest fancied stealing a feather for herself. *I shall find an opportunity to pull out a feather*, she thought, and she kept a watchful eye. As soon as the youngest brother left the goose in the stable, she seized it by its wings. But, noticing something strange, she quickly tried to let go again and found that her hand was stuck fast! Soon she heard a noise at the door and started to panic, fearing that she was about to be found out, but it was just her sister. This sister had also sought a golden feather. On seeing her eldest sister looking so alarmed she immediately tried to help her, but as soon as she touched her sister's arm she found that she too was stuck. At last the third sister also came to the room, with the very same intent as the others. This time the two stuck-together sisters tried to dissuade her. "Keep away, for goodness' sake, keep away!" they cried, but she didn't understand why and rushed toward her sisters regardless. Soon enough, she too was stuck. Now the youngest sister was stuck to the middle sister and the middle sister was stuck to the eldest sister and the eldest sister was stuck to the goose! That night they all had no choice but to sleep in the stable.

The following morning, the brother went to the stable for the goose, picked it up and put it under his arm, not stopping to wonder why there were three girls attached to it. Off he went, beginning his walk home, and the sisters followed him, for they could do nothing else. As they crossed the fields behind the inn they came across a parson. “My dear girls,” he said, “why are you chasing after this young man so?” And he reached out to catch the arm of the youngest daughter so that she may answer his question. Well! He soon found out that the girls were following the brother because they were all stuck to one another – and now that the parson had touched them, he was also stuck. The same thing happened to the sexton as he tried to catch the parson by the sleeve. Not only that, but when they passed a pair of labourers the parson foolishly called out for help and before they knew it both labourers were stuck too. And so there walked a truly surprising procession, with sisters one, two and three, the parson, the sexton and not one but two labourers all in a line together, trailing after the youngest brother and the goose.

After some time they reached a city ruled by a king whose daughter was so serious that she *never* laughed. When the youngest brother heard of this, he went to the princess and stood before her, with the train of people behind him. As soon as the princess saw the seven people running after the brother she began to laugh very loudly. In fact, it sounded as though she might never stop. As he had succeeded in making her laugh, the king decreed that the youngest brother be rewarded with enough wealth to make sure that he lived comfortably for the rest of his days. On his return home, his father declared how proud he was of his youngest son, and promised to never underestimate him again.

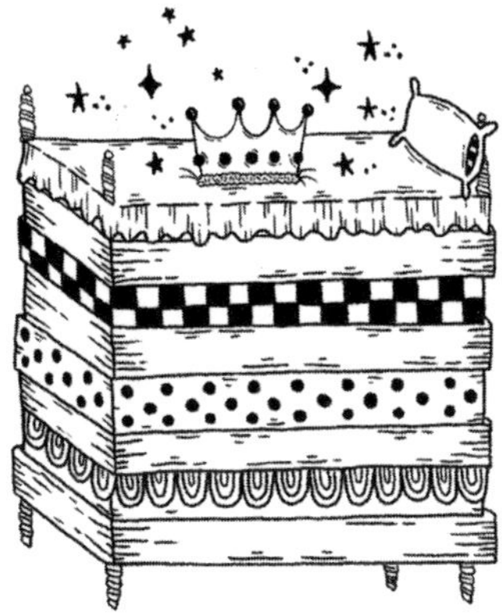

The Princess and the Pea

Written by Hans Christian Andersen, "The Princess and the Pea" was first published alongside three other tales in a small booklet in 1835. However, the story itself had existed for many years before Andersen put pen to paper – indeed, in the preface of the second volume of *Tales and Stories* that was published in 1865, Andersen said that he had originally heard the story in his childhood. In Italy, a similar story was passed down through generations, called "The Most Sensitive Woman".

Once upon a time, there lived a prince. The prince lived in the royal palace with his mother and father, helping them rule over their kingdom kindly and fairly. After many years looking for someone to fall in love with, the prince was starting to think that perhaps they did not exist. You see, the law decreed that the prince could only marry a princess, for only a true princess could be worthy of a prince.

One dark and stormy night, as rain thrashed loudly against the grand stately windows, a *knock-knock-knock* could be heard. Someone was at the palace door.

"Who could that be, to visit us in the middle of the night?" asked the queen. The footman rushed to the door, and upon opening it saw a young woman, drenched from head to toe from the rain.

"I'm so sorry to disturb you," she said, as rain dripped from her hair. "I was thrown from my horse and became quite lost. Please, could I stay here for the night?"

As the prince looked upon the woman, he felt a rush of affection for her. "Of course, you must stay," he replied, and the woman smiled. "We will prepare a room for you at once." While servants rushed to light a fire and make up a bed in one of the guest rooms, the queen led the young woman to the drawing room so that she may sit by the fire. "Where are you from?" she asked, to which the woman replied that she lived in a kingdom quite far away. The queen was quiet for a moment, deep in thought. "You look so familiar…" she said at last. "Have we ever met?" But the woman insisted this could not be so. "I am not used to being in royal company," she replied, although the queen noticed that she looked at the floor as she did so. Soon it was announced that the room was ready. "Perhaps you could sit here a while longer," said the queen. "You must still be feeling extremely cold after getting caught in such a storm. I'm sure my son would be most happy to wait up with you awhile," she added. The prince smiled in agreement, and upon seeing his kindness the woman smiled too.

Once the queen had left the drawing room, she went up to the guest room that had been so carefully prepared – and on her way, she stopped at the kitchen. You see, the queen was a very clever woman, and very intuitive too. While the young woman had said that she knew not of any royal families, there was something about her – her kind nature, her politeness, and the way she held herself – that told the queen otherwise. While in the kitchen, the queen plucked a single pea from the cook's pantry and took it to the guest bedroom.

Once upstairs, the queen ordered the servants to bring more mattresses. "I need twenty at least," she cried, and of course her servants obeyed. On top of the mattresses, the servants also placed twenty quilts filled with the softest of feathers. Once they were done, the queen carefully placed the single pea under the bottom-most mattress. And with that, the queen retired to her chambers.

In the morning, the royal family sat down to breakfast with their guest. The storm had quietened soon after the woman's arrival, so the king, queen and prince had all benefitted from a glorious night of sleep. Their guest, however, looked extremely tired. "My dear," said the queen, "did you sleep well?"

"I'm afraid I did not," said the woman with embarrassment. "I'm very sorry to say that my bed was awfully uncomfortable – I could feel something digging into me all night, and I appear to be bruised all over this morning." At this, the queen knew that her instincts had been right – it was not just any young woman who sat before them, it was a princess! No other being would have skin so sensitive that they felt a single pea through twenty mattresses and twenty feather quilts! When she kindly said as much, the woman admitted the truth. "I am indeed a princess," she said, "but my parents were forcing me to marry someone with whom I was not in love. So I ran away in the hope that I could keep my identity a secret."

In this moment, the king and queen realized the error of their ways – in telling the prince that he may only marry a princess, they were making him deeply unhappy. And so it was decreed that the prince should be able to marry whomever he pleased – whether they were of royal blood or not. As news travelled across the lands, kings and queens of other kingdoms chose to do the same – even the princess's own mother and father, who had of course missed her terribly. The prince and princess rejoiced in this news, and remained friends for many years, never forgetting the change that had come as a result of their first encounter.

Jack and the Beanstalk

"Jack and the Beanstalk" is an English fairy tale. Originally called "The Story of Jack Spriggins and the Enchanted Bean", it can be dated back to around 1734. Adapted to "The History of Jack and the Bean-Stalk" by Benjamin Tabart in 1807, the tale was featured within a book called *The Home Treasury* in 1845 and then rewritten again, this time by Joseph Jacobs, to be included in *English Fairy Tales* in 1890.

In a land far away, in a small cottage on a small farm, lived a young boy called Jack and his mother, Mary. Jack's father had passed away long ago, and he and his mother had become very poor. They lived a simple life and the only thing of real value that they owned was a cow, whose milk they sold so that they had enough money to feed themselves.

One day, Jack's mother came to him looking very sad.

"The cow has stopped making milk," she said. "Now all we have to sell is the cow herself. Take her to the market, Jack, and get a good price. The money you get in return is all we will have in the world."

Jack set off for the market that afternoon, feeling a bit annoyed about having to walk such a long way. But it wasn't long before he came across a man selling wares by the roadside.

"Beans for sale!" he called, as Jack approached with the cow.

"Beans?" said Jack. "Who would want to spend their money on *beans*?"

The man explained that these weren't just any old beans. "They're magic!" he said. Now, Jack had never heard of *magic* beans before, but now that he had he knew that he wanted some! Before he could stop to think, he had agreed to trade the cow for a handful of beans, and as he waved goodbye to the man he felt enormously pleased with himself.

Once home, he sat down at the kitchen table to inspect his magic beans.

"Back so soon?" asked his mother, as she came in from clearing the cow's stable. "How much money were you able to get for the cow?"

"Oh, I didn't get *money*, Mother," said Jack, still feeling very pleased. "I got *beans*. *Magic beans*!"

Well! You can probably imagine how cross Jack's mother was. Now they didn't have a penny in the world – how on earth would they buy food? In her anger, Jack's mother grabbed the handful of beans and threw them out of the window before sending Jack straight to bed without any dinner. Of course, she went to bed without dinner too, as Jack hadn't brought home any money.

That night, while Jack's mother dreamt worried dreams and Jack slept soundly in his bed, something unusual was happening just outside their windows.

At first there was just the tiniest shoot breaking through the soil, but one stalk turned to two and two stalks turned to four, and so it went. Each stalk was immensely thick, and as they intertwined a giant beanstalk was formed.

The following morning, Jack rose early to start his chores. He wasn't normally very good at being helpful but he thought he'd make a special effort, as his mother had been so cross about the beans. However, when Jack looked out of his window he was surprised to see an enormous beanstalk growing from the ground. He rushed outside and stood at the bottom of it. It was almost as wide as their house, and it reached up into the sky as far as the eye could see!

But what is at the top? wondered Jack to himself. Maybe food, or another cow … or maybe even gold! Before he could think twice, Jack started climbing. If he brought back some gold for his mother then she would surely be happy with him.

Up and up Jack climbed, for *miles* it seemed. It took him so long that he thought about turning back. But he kept going. And finally Jack reached the top.

Looking around, Jack found himself in a strange

country – one he had never seen before. He saw a long road stretching ahead of him, and he started to make his way down it. It wasn't long before he noticed a woman sitting by the roadside.

She was very small and wore a hooded cloak that was tattered and torn.

She must be poor, thought Jack.

As the woman saw Jack passing by, she stood up from her perch. Seeing that she was eager to speak to him, Jack approached her cautiously.

The woman sighed deeply. "Jack," she said. "You're finally here."

Jack was shocked – how did this woman know his name? He asked her as much, and she looked at him quite curiously, as if to check that it really was him after all. After a moment, she nodded her head slightly and asked Jack to join her sitting on the perch, for she had a tale to tell him.

"Many years ago, a man, his wife and their baby boy lived happily. The man and his wife were known throughout the land for being both kind and fair, and because of this they were beloved. Through their hard work they amassed enormous wealth, and this too was widely known, as they shared their wealth to help many people.

"It so happened that a giant lived many miles away, but whereas the man was kind and fair, the giant was greedy and cruel. He heard stories of the man's riches and decided that he wanted those riches for himself, so embarked on a journey to the man's abode. Once there, the giant spun an elaborate tale, telling the man that he had lost his home and belongings in a terrible earthquake. The man of course wanted to help the giant, as he did not suspect his treachery. And so he allowed the giant to stay in his house as an honoured guest.

"But as soon as the man went to his study that first night, the giant found him there and stabbed him thrice in the back. The man called out in pain, and shouted for his wife to escape, for his first thought was for their safety. He died within moments, but his heart's wish was granted – for his wife heeded his calls, and ran with their baby son to hide.

"The giant searched and searched for them, but for the life of him he could not find them. He decided to leave the dwelling, for fear of being caught, but before he left he was sure to take all of the family's gold, silverware and jewels, for that was the reason behind his murderous act.

"Though the giant went back to his own faraway

land, the woman knew that she could no longer live with her son in their home, for she would always fear that the giant would return. So she waited patiently in her hiding place, cradling her child close to her breast, until she was sure that the giant was gone. And then she stole away into the night, never to be seen again."

As the woman came to the end of her story, she looked at Jack knowingly, and at once Jack saw what she was telling him: the man in the story was his father, the woman was his mother, and Jack himself was the baby that was protected so dearly.

"This land you have come to is the giant's land," said the woman, "and the castle in which he now lives with his wife is just yonder." She pointed into the distance, and Jack followed her gaze to see a large castle near the end of the long and winding road.

The woman continued. "Every treasure the giant owns was first stolen from your father and mother, and rightfully belongs to you. Though it would be terribly dangerous, you could claim the riches back if you so choose." Filled with anger for the horrible end his father had met at the hands of the giant, Jack immediately resolved to seek revenge for his dear mother who had protected him for so many years. With one nod, he left the woman and embarked on his long journey along the road.

After a while he came across an enormous house, with steps as tall as tables and a doorway as tall as a house. Not long before, Jack would have boldly walked inside, for he had been a silly boy who didn't fear anything. But now he knew the truth about his past he became cautious. He would not be betrayed as his father had been. Jack crept quietly inside, but quickly came across a giant woman.

"My goodness," she said, "a human child! You mustn't be here – my husband is coming home soon and he will certainly eat you if he finds you here."

"Please," said Jack. "I have travelled so far and am awfully hungry. If you could spare something small for me to eat and drink, I would be ever so grateful."

The giant woman thought for a moment and then let out a sigh. "All right," she said, as she prepared him some bread, cheese and milk. Jack feasted on the food, for climbing up the beanstalk had been hard work indeed. He was about to ask for some more when he heard an almighty *THUMP! THUMP!*

THUMP! coming from close by.

"My husband!" cried the woman. "Quick, you must hide!"

She ushered Jack into the oven and there he hid, as quiet as a mouse.

No sooner had the giant woman closed the oven door, than an even bigger giant did emerge.

"Hello, Wife," he started to say as he walked into the room, but he stopped himself short and sniffed the air.

"I smell fresh human," he said loudly.

"There is no human here," said his wife. "That must be yesterday's dinner that you can smell." And to distract her husband, the woman giant brought him three large bags of gold coins to count. Suitably distracted, the giant man sat at the table to count his money. Jack eyed the gold longingly from his hiding place in the oven. Now that he knew the gold had belonged to his father, he resolved that he would take it back. It wasn't long before the giant's eyes grew heavy and he fell into a deep sleep, snoring loudly.

The giant woman rushed to open the oven, instructing Jack to leave right away. Jack did as he was told, but not before stealing a large bag of gold coins from the giant's table while the woman's back was turned.

Off Jack ran to the beanstalk, and down, down he climbed. When he reached the bottom, he called for his mother and showed her the bulging bag of gold coins. When Jack told his mother what he had been told, she gasped in shock, for she had always been too scared to tell Jack about his father and the giant who had betrayed him. "Oh, Jack, promise me you will not go back," she said. "I am truly grateful for the gold that you brought back to me – the riches that I once lost – but you are worth more than any gold. That giant is wicked. Please, do not risk your life again."

Jack agreed, for he did not wish to cause his mother worry, and for a number of years Jack and his mother lived happily and comfortably. They were careful with their gold coins, and used them sparingly, as they did not wish to become poor again, so Jack had no reason to climb the beanstalk. And yet he found himself thinking of it often, and one evening, after his mother had fallen asleep, he packed a bag and climbed back up the beanstalk.

Somehow the journey seemed quicker the second time, and it wasn't long before Jack reached the top. The woman was no longer there, but the road that led to the giant's house looked exactly as it had before. As he approached the house for the second time, Jack kept a careful watch. But just like last time he found the giant's wife alone, and also just like last time he asked if she could spare him some food. The giant's wife agreed, but as she was preparing the food she suddenly remembered that a bag of gold coins had gone missing the last time Jack had been there.

"Do you know what happened to it?" she implored.

"Certainly not," said Jack, in what he hoped was a convincing way, and the giant woman looked at him for a long while, as if to decide whether she believed him or not. However, she didn't have a chance to question him further before they heard the familiar *THUMP! THUMP! THUMP!* of the giant man's footsteps. This time the giant woman rushed Jack into the lumber closet, and he had only just got inside when the giant came crashing through the door, shouting that he could smell a human.

"There, there," said his wife, as she settled him at the table. "There is no human here. But let me fetch your golden goose while you sit here resting. I know how it relaxes you so." Off she went to another room, returning with the most curious goose Jack had ever seen. It was the same size and shape as a normal goose, but it had the most glorious gold feathers.

The giant observed the golden goose for a moment, and then said, "Lay!" in a very loud voice. To Jack's surprise, the goose not only obeyed the command but laid a *golden* egg.

Knowing that the giant would fall asleep before long, Jack waited patiently for his chance. As soon as he heard the giant's snores he climbed up on to the table and stole the golden goose, running away as fast as his legs would carry him.

Back at home, his mother smiled with delight at the beautiful goose her son had brought back to her. Of course, she knew exactly how to request the golden eggs, as the goose had long before belonged to her and her husband. But despite her happiness at being reunited with her family treasure, she did caution Jack.

"You mustn't climb back up the beanstalk ever again," she very seriously. "Golden goose or no golden goose, it's a dangerous place up there and you must not risk your life."

Jack agreed, and in that moment he truly meant it, but as time passed he found himself thinking once more of the giant's house at the top of the beanstalk, and seven nights later he decided to visit it one last time.

Once again Jack climbed the beanstalk, and once again he walked along the quiet road to the giant's house. But this time, when he arrived, the giant's wife was nowhere to be seen. Jack hesitated at the door, wondering if he should go in, before stepping over the threshold. This time, he had only been in the house for a matter of seconds before he heard the terrifying *THUMP! THUMP! THUMP!* of the giant's footsteps. With no time to spare, he jumped into a nearby copper pot and sat trembling inside it.

"I smell a HUMAN!" Jack heard the giant shout, and he carefully peered out of the pot to see the giant sniffing the air with his enormous nose. As quick as a flash, the giant ran to the oven and peered inside. Did he know that Jack had hidden there before? After searching the inside of the oven thoroughly, the giant sat down at his kitchen table and produced an exquisite harp.

Putting his feet up on the chair opposite him, the giant made himself comfortable before shouting,

"Play!" at the harp. To Jack's wonder, the harp started to play the most mesmerizing music all by itself.

And before he knew it, Jack's mind was made up: he would steal the harp.

To Jack's relief, the giant fell asleep much more quickly than before. Jack crept silently across the giant's kitchen floor and climbed on to the tabletop where the magical harp stood. But when Jack grabbed the harp and started his escape:

"Master! Master!" called the harp to the giant. "Master!"

The giant awoke, groggy from his slumber and still half asleep. By the time he realized what had happened, Jack was well on his way back to the beanstalk. Climbing down the stalk frantically, with the harp crying out loudly, Jack cursed his own curiosity.

I should have listened to my dear mother! he thought. Above him, he heard the almighty crashing of leaves as the giant made his way down the beanstalk. Thankfully, Jack was nimble and knew the beanstalk well, so he climbed down it much faster than the giant. As Jack neared the bottom he called to his mother, saying,

"Mother! Mother! Bring out the axe!" Luckily for Jack, his mother was a quick-thinking woman, and on hearing her son's distressed voice she grabbed two axes from their woodshed and stood ready at the bottom of the stalk. As soon as Jack was safely on the ground, he and his mother started chopping at the beanstalk with strong, quick blows.

Chop! Chop! Chop!

High above them, the giant felt the beanstalk shudder and shake, and miles below, as Jack and his mother delivered their final blows, they cut clear through the beanstalk, sending it crashing to the ground.

The giant was never to be seen again.

From that day on, while Jack often thought about the beanstalk and the giant's house, he never did go back to the strange land. Instead, he and his mother lived contentedly in their little cottage for the rest of their days.

Beauty and the Beast

First written by Gabrielle-Suzanne Barbot de Villeneuve and published in 1740 as part of *The Young American and Marine Tales*, "La Belle et la Bête", as it is known in France, is one of the most popular fairy tales known today. The original version, which was rather long, was abridged and rewritten by Jeanne-Marie Leprince de Beaumont in 1756, and included in *The Children's Collection*. A version also appears in Andrew Lang's *Blue Fairy Book* which first published in 1889.

Many years ago, in a far-off country, a man lived with his six daughters and six sons. The man was a merchant, and through hard work and some luck, he had become very rich indeed. The family lived together in a beautiful house in the centre of a busy town. The merchant's children had, over the years, become used to his wealth and the luxuries it afforded them. They did not want for anything, as they already had even more than they could possibly hope for.

But misfortunes befell them.

One day, a fire started within their family home. While they were all able to escape unscathed, their clothes, photographs, books, furniture, and all of their most treasured belongings were lost within the fire. Faced with this adversity, the merchant tried to reassure his children. "We still have my fleet of ships," he said. "They are all at sea, upon various journeys, but when they return some of our wealth will be restored to us."

But this would not come to pass, as at the very same time that their beloved home was burnt to the ground, the entire fleet of ships that the merchant owned was destroyed in a terrible storm across the seas. While the family had before known great wealth, they were now thrown into a poverty of which they had never before experienced.

The merchant was fortunate to own a small cottage many miles away from the town and so he moved his family there. While his sons and daughters tried their very best to stay positive for their father, they found this task very hard indeed. They missed the friends they had been forced to leave behind, and though they had hoped to be visited at the cottage, or invited to stay at one of the grand properties in the town, it seemed that their friends had disappeared along with their wealth and good fortune.

Their cottage stood in the midst of a forest, and at first seemed like a rather dismal place. But the children did what they could to brighten it and make it feel like home. Still, the family was so poor that everyone needed to work, and they all either secured employment or tended the land surrounding the cottage, growing fruit and vegetables to eat and sell. Roughly clothed and living in the simplest way, all of the children soon realized just how lucky they had been before.

At this time, there was one of the merchant's children who worked even harder than her brothers and sisters: Beauty. Beauty was named so because of her kind face and resilient nature, as she was beautiful both inside and out. When her siblings struggled with the hand that fate had dealt them, Beauty was always able to cheer them up by reminding them of all that they still had – the roof over their heads, the well that supplied fresh water, the lush garden that had already started to bear vegetables. Beauty's brothers and sisters were grateful for her dutiful love and support.

After some time, news reached them that one of the merchant's ships had actually survived the terrible storm and had come safely into port bearing a rich cargo. The family rejoiced for this good fortune, and the merchant prepared to set off as soon as possible to travel to the town and reclaim his ship. As he got on his horse, he asked each of his children what they would like him to bring them when he returned. They all asked for some luxurious item or another – all, that is, except for Beauty, who instead asked her father to bring her back a rose. "Is that really all that you desire?" he asked in surprise, and Beauty reassured him. She had become used to their new life, and the lives they had once lived now seemed quite empty to her. But no roses grew in their garden or the forest that surrounded it, and how she longed to see a rose again. Her father agreed to bring one back for her, and off he went.

The merchant reached the town as quickly as possible, but his good mood was soon replaced with anger, as he found that the ship's cargo had already been divided. His former colleagues claimed that they had thought him to be dead because they had heard no word from him. Not knowing whether to believe them, the merchant saw that there was nothing he could do. With a heavy heart, he started his journey home.

When the merchant was but halfway into his journey, the weather became cold and harsh. *Should I turn back?* he wondered, but when it started to snow he realized that his only choice was to continue forward. Night set in and darkness fell, and not one house was seen. The only shelter the merchant could find was the hollow of a tree trunk, within which he crouched for some time and tried to shelter his horse as best he could. But upon hearing the howling of wolves, the merchant climbed back on his horse and rode on.

Not knowing which way to turn, the merchant tried his best to navigate, and soon found that he was riding upon a road. To his surprise, after a short while the road led him to an avenue of orange trees that led in turn to a splendid castle. Though the merchant had ridden through snow and ice, no snow fell upon the castle grounds – in fact, the trees were in full bloom, with branches bowing beneath the weight of the fruit and flowers that were growing in abundance. "Why, it's as if I have ridden into another world," exclaimed the merchant to himself, as he rode down the avenue beneath the moonlight. He came to a stable, where fresh food and water was lying in wait for his horse, and upon leading his horse there to rest awhile, the merchant walked up to the castle door, which groaned loudly as he pushed it open. *It is as if this door has been neither opened nor closed in many years*, he thought.

Walking through the castle, the merchant took care to look into each room. Each one appeared entirely deserted. Indeed, the merchant did not see even one person as he made his way around the castle. After some time, he came across a small room in which an inviting fire was roaring within a fireplace. Drawn to the warmth, the merchant moved closer, and as he did so he noticed a small table set in front of a comfortable chair. The table had a delicious meal set out upon it, and at once the merchant started eating, so hungry was he from his long and treacherous journey. When finished, he sat and waited for his host to appear so that he may thank them for their generosity. But the host never came, and after some waiting the merchant began to feel extremely tired. He sat back in the chair, and fell into a deep sleep.

When the merchant awoke, it was the middle of the night and the castle was still silent. Not one soul had appeared. While he had hoped to say thank you for the food and warmth bestowed upon him, he decided to ready himself to leave, as the quietness of such a large castle was starting to scare him somewhat. To be sure that the host was not there, the merchant resolved to look once more in all of the rooms he had passed. Still they remained empty. "Such a curious place," he remarked as he closed the heavy door behind him. He was about to walk into the stable when he noticed a rosebush filled with the most beautiful roses he had ever come across. Breathing in their heavy scent, he remembered

Beauty's request and reached out to pluck the most beautiful rose he could see.

All of a sudden, the merchant became aware of a noise behind him, and when he turned around he was startled to see the most frightful beast. Calling out in alarm, he tried to back away, but fell to the ground, which only served to make the beast look even larger and more frightening.

"You dare to assume that you may take one of my roses?" the Beast shouted in anger. "Was it not enough that I gave you shelter and warmth, and food to eat – you felt the need to steal from me as well?"

The merchant was terrified, and cowered so. "Please, noble sir, pardon me. I am truly grateful for your hospitality and kindness, and did not intend to insult you. Please, forgive me." But the Beast's anger was not lessened by the merchant's words. "Your excuses and flattery do not mean a thing," he declared. "And they will not save you from punishment." Upon hearing these words, fear rose up within the merchant and he started to speak desperately, telling the Beast of his loss of fortune and the failed journey he had made to the town. "I became lost!" he cried. "I did not know! I simply picked the rose to give to my dear daughter, Beauty."

At once the Beast quietened, seeming much calmer than before. "You have a daughter?" he asked quietly. "Indeed, sir – I have six," the merchant replied, "and six sons as well. They wait at home for me and I pray that I may see them again."

After some thought, the Beast turned to the merchant. "I will forgive you for your behaviour," he said, "if you agree to one thing: give me one of your children so that they may stay here in your place."

The merchant was horrified. "I couldn't possibly!" he cried, but even as he said the words he knew that he had no choice. Some of his children were quite young and could not look after themselves – what would happen to them if their father were never to return? He turned to the Beast. "But what excuse could I invent to bring one of my children here?" he asked wearily.

"You must not lie," said the Beast. "If one of your children comes at all, they must do so willingly. You must see if any of them are courageous enough to save your life. On no other condition will they be welcome. You seem to be an honest man," the Beast continued, "so I will trust you to go home. I give you one month to see if any of your children are willing to take your place. If none of them is willing, you must return here alone. And do not imagine that you can hide from me," said the Beast in a low growl. "If you fail to keep your word, I will find you."

The merchant found himself accepting the Beast's proposal and asked to set off at once, so anxious was he at spending even a moment longer in this place. "You may leave on the morrow," said the Beast. "You may only rise when you see the sun and hear a golden bell ring. You will find breakfast waiting for you. Once you have eaten, you will see a horse waiting for you in the courtyard. You may ride this horse home, and if one of your children shall agree to this bargain, then you will return with them on the same horse." The Beast reminded the merchant of his promise and warned him to be truthful with his children. "Take this rose to Beauty," he said finally, handing him a most beautiful bloom, "and in the morning, be gone!"

That night, the merchant lay down on the comfortable bed and, despite feeling that he couldn't possibly sleep, he fell into the deepest sleep he had ever known.

The next morning, he did everything as the Beast had instructed, and once he had mounted the horse it carried him away so swiftly that the castle soon became but a speck in the distance behind them. The merchant was so lost within his own gloomy thoughts that he was quite startled when he saw his home in the distance. It felt as if the journey had taken no time at all.

The merchant's sons and daughters rushed to meet him with such happiness on their faces. He had been gone so long that they had feared the worst. But their happiness turned to horror as he told them of what he had experienced, and no one felt more terribly than poor Beauty. "If only I had not asked for a rose," she said quietly, but her father would not accept this, and said over and over that it was not her fault. Still, Beauty did not agree. "I will stay with the Beast in your place, Father," she said, and they could all see how fiercely she meant it. Her father tried to argue, and her sisters and brothers too, but Beauty was firm and soon they saw that she would not be dissuaded. She divided the little belongings she had amassed amongst them all, and spent the day enjoying their company. As night started to fall, she mounted the horse with her father. As the horse started to gallop, it felt more as if it were flying, and so smoothly did it move that Beauty felt oddly calm. When she spied the avenue of orange trees that her father had described, she knew that they were almost there – and at this point Beauty did feel anxious indeed, for she did not know what lay ahead of her. In spite of her anxiety, Beauty was able to look at her surroundings with wonder. She lifted her face towards the orange trees as she rode between them, catching their sweet scent, and was sure she could hear faint music coming from within the castle.

When they had dismounted, the merchant led Beauty to the small room that he had first gone to, and they found a splendid fire burning there for them. They sat down to wait, and it was not long before they heard the Beast's heavy footsteps along the corridor. Beauty clung to her father in fear, and felt all the more scared when she realized how frightened he was. But when the Beast stepped into the room, Beauty took great effort to calm her trembling and not seem afraid of him. The Beast looked upon her and at once knew that she was the Beauty of which her father had spoken. "Good evening, old man. Good evening, Beauty," he said with a growl, and though her father was too terrified to reply, Beauty stepped forward. "Good evening, Beast," she said, with as much courage as she possessed. Her boldness seemed to satisfy the Beast, who went on to ask if she had come to the castle willingly. "Will you be content to stay here while your father goes?" he asked intently, to which Beauty replied, "Yes."

"Then I am pleased," said the Beast. "As you have come of your own accord, then you can stay."

The Beast turned to the merchant and fixed him with his gaze. "You will depart at sunrise tomorrow," he said. "When the bell rings, you may rise for breakfast and you will find the horse waiting for you once you have eaten your fill. The horse will take you home." The Beast started to turn away but paused, as if a thought had occurred to him. "Say your goodbyes now, and remember: you must never expect to see my castle again," he said quietly, and with that he left the room.

Beauty and her father dined together that night, and stayed up very late speaking of many things. For they knew that, come the morning, they would likely never see one another ever again.

When Beauty retired to the room that was to be hers, she was struck by its opulence. The bed sheets were made of the softest silk and the mattress was so comfortable that when she lay down Beauty sank straight into a deep sleep. In her sleep, Beauty started to dream. She dreamt that she was walking beside a pretty brook bordered by flowers. Lamenting her terrible fate, she sat down and started to cry. "You are not so unfortunate as you imagine," said a voice, startling her at first, and Beauty looked up to see a prince. He looked at her kindly. "Here you will find many things that your heart desires," said the prince, "so do not be sad. In your own happiness, you may well find mine – you may be able to set me free. Please, Beauty, find me, no matter how I may be disguised. Only someone as true-hearted as you can do this." No sooner had the prince finished speaking than Beauty found herself in a room, standing before a handsome woman. "Dear Beauty," she said, "try not to dwell on all you have left behind and do not let yourself be deceived by appearances. For things are rarely quite as they seem."

Beauty found her dreams so curious that she was in no rush to wake, but presently she was roused from slumber by a clock softly calling her name twelve times.

As she readied herself for the day ahead, she thought back upon her dream. *Perhaps the prince is a prisoner here*, she mused, *held captive by the beast*. But although she knew the beast to look quite fearsome, she did not believe him to be cruel. Convincing herself that her dream was just that – a dream and nothing more – Beauty resolved to explore the castle, as she quite simply had nothing else to do. As she walked down a particular corridor, Beauty came across a series of doors. Behind the first she found a room lined with many mirrors. She walked through it, seeing herself reflected in the mirrors one hundred times over. Light streamed in through the windows and was captured by each of the mirrors bearing her reflection. Why! She had never come across such a charming room! As she was about to exit, she noticed a small bracelet hanging from a chandelier, and, to her surprise, when Beauty took it in her hand she saw that the bracelet held a portrait of the prince she had seen in her dream. Opening the clasp, Beauty carefully put the bracelet upon her wrist and continued her exploration. The next room was a gallery of paintings, and Beauty gasped when she saw that the largest painting of all was a portrait of the prince. At first she thought that she must be mistaken, but she studied it closely and became quite sure. The man in the portrait really did look like the man from her dream, and he appeared to be smiling at her kindly. Tearing herself away from the portrait at last, Beauty walked into a room that contained every musical instrument ever known, and beyond that room Beauty found herself within the most magnificent library. As she traced the spines with her fingers and breathed in the musky smell of the books, Beauty noticed that the books were all those that she either deeply wanted to read, or had already read and loved. *What a truly magical library, to contain so many of my desires*, she thought.

As Beauty put her hand on the handle of the next door, she realized that she was starting to feel hungry, so when she opened the door to see a delicious supper laid out for her she was quite amazed. All day she had not seen one person or heard one sound. Though she had come to the castle willingly, she had already started to feel lonely. As she walked over to the table she noticed that darkness was falling outside of the castle, and she heard the heavy steps that told her the Beast was on his way. "Good evening, Beauty," he said as he entered the room, and again Beauty managed to reply politely despite her fear. They ate together and talked for a while, with beauty telling the Beast all she had seen that day.

After some time, the Beast got up to leave and said a kind, "Good night."

"Good night, Beast," said Beauty in return and she hastened to her room, eager to fall asleep and dream of the prince.

In her dream, the prince spoke to Beauty once more. "I fear I am fated to live out my days unhappily," he confided as they walked amongst the most beautiful gardens.

When morning came, Beauty's first thought was to return to the portrait to see if it really was her prince who was painted there. She found the likeness to be exact, which further threw her into a state of confusion. As the sun shone brightly from outside, she resolved to take in some air, and she wandered outside to explore the castle grounds. Once outside, Beauty was astonished to find that every place she walked was already familiar to her, and presently she came across a brook surrounded by flowers that looked just like the one from her dream. "It is exactly as it was when I first met the prince," she said aloud.

She thought again to the prince and whether the Beast could have imprisoned him, but, again, she felt in her heart that this was not the case.

The days passed swiftly, and Beauty found that there were many ways for her to pass the time within the castle grounds. She learned much from all of the books she read, and was able to partake in a number of creative pursuits, such was the vastness of the castle and the incredible contents of each and every room. Though Beauty never saw the Beast during the day, each evening he would appear at sundown and sup with her. During these times their conversations were interesting, and Beauty found that the Beast was both kind-hearted and considerate. As the days and evenings passed, Beauty realized that she had started to see the Beast as something more than his hideous form. She had started to see him as a dear friend. Every night Beauty would meet with the prince in her dreams, and with every meeting she would learn something new about him. The only thing that disturbed her was the prince's insistence that she must not trust appearances, but when she pressed him on the meaning of this he was unable to say.

For a long while, everything went on just like this, but while Beauty had initially been able to stop herself thinking about her family, there came a time when she started to feel overwhelmed with sadness, such was her loss. One evening, upon seeing her look so sad, the Beast asked Beauty what was wrong. By now, Beauty knew the Beast well enough that she was able to tell him the truth without fearing reproach, and so she did so kindly.

"I am grateful for everything that you have bestowed upon me," said Beauty, "But I am filled with a deep yearning to see my family. I understand that this is not possible, for it is not the agreement that I made with you, but it fills me with such sadness to know that I shall never see my family again."

When Beauty had finished speaking, the Beast was quiet for a long time, and she feared that she had offended him deeply, but when he spoke it was with soft words. "I would not want to refuse you anything in this life," he said, and Beauty knew it to be true. "You may return to your family, but, please, I beg you, do not be gone for more than two months, for I fear the consequences will be great if you are. When you wish to come back, you will not need a horse or a chariot to return; simply say the words 'I wish to go back to my castle and see my Beast again' aloud, and you shall return here. Good night, Beauty. Fear nothing, and sleep peacefully, for before long you shall see your family once more."

That night, Beauty fell into a happy sleep, and looked forward to telling her prince the good news. But when she found him in her dream he seemed most unlike himself. "My prince, whatever is the matter," Beauty asked, to which the prince admitted that he would miss her. "I worry that I will never see you again," he said with sadness. "Please, don't be so full of sorrow," Beauty replied, and she took his hand in hers. "I have promised the Beast that I shall return, and he would be terribly sad if I did not keep my word."

"Does the opinion of this Beast mean so much to you?" asked the prince thoughtfully, and Beauty realized that, yes, it did. "I care for the Beast very much," she said, "and I have found him to be both kind and gentle."

With that a strange sound awoke her, as if someone was speaking to her from far away, and Beauty opened her eyes to find that she was back in the cottage where her father lived with her brothers and sisters. They were all astonished to see her when she rushed out of the room that used to be hers, and there seemed no end to the questions that they asked her. More than anything they were relieved to find her safe and happy. "Does this mean you have returned home for good?" her father asked, but Beauty fell quiet.

"I'm sorry, Father, but no," she said eventually. "I made a promise to the Beast and, more than that, I wish to return to him." Though her family were surprised at Beauty's words and tried to convince her to stay, they also knew that she was strong of heart, and finally they agreed to be happy for her temporary return and make the most of the limited time that they had with her.

As days passed, Beauty found that she felt much changed by her time with the Beast, and she noticed that her family had also changed in her absence. She missed the Beast, and also the prince – whom she had not dreamt about since her return – and she found herself yearning for her life at the castle. But Beauty also enjoyed the company of her family so much that each night, instead of returning to the Beast, she resolved to put it off for just one more day. This continued for many nights, until Beauty had been with her family for almost two months. But one night, as Beauty slept, she dreamt that she was wandering along a lonely path in the castle gardens. Suddenly she heard a cry, and upon following the sound she came across the Beast stretched out upon his side and in great pain. "Beauty!" he called out when he saw her, and when she heard his voice Beauty felt something stir deep within her. Waking from her dream with a start, Beauty knew that she could wait no longer. "I wish to go back to my castle and see my Beast again," she said quickly. And with that she fell fast asleep.

"Beauty, Beauty," said the clock twelve times, and Beauty knew that she was in the castle once more. Every room looked the same as before, with everything just as she had left it. Knowing that the Beast would not appear before supper, Beauty waited for him patiently, but the hour came and went, and still the Beast did not arrive. Beauty felt panic start to swell inside her and, not knowing what else to do, she rushed outside to the gardens. Would the Beast be in the place she had dreamt? Up and down the paths she ran, calling his name. But no one answered. Finally, she was forced to stop to catch her breath and, looking up, realized that she was standing opposite the shaded path from her dream. Forgetting her fatigue, she ran down it and – sure enough – there lay the Beast. Was he sleeping? She did not know, but she cradled him in her arms and stroked his head.

"Dear Beast," she cried, "please, do not leave me. For, I have realized that I love you." As she watched him closely, with tears falling down her face, she was amazed to see that he was still breathing. To Beauty's great delight, the Beast started to revive.

"Can you really love such an ugly creature as I?" he asked, when his strength had returned. "Yes, dear Beast," she said in reply. And in that moment a blaze of light shone so brightly that Beauty had to shield her eyes. When she felt able to look again, Beauty saw that the Beast had disappeared, and in his place stood the prince from her dreams. "Am I dreaming?" asked Beauty, and the prince smiled. "My dear Beauty," he said, "you have rescued me from a terrible enchantment and restored me to my natural form."

In that moment, the woman from Beauty's dream appeared. She was a fairy who had been trying to aid the prince in breaking the enchantment. "Beauty, you had courage where no other person did," she said, "and you learned a lesson that many do not: that it is not what we see on the outside that counts, but what we know to be on the inside."

Hansel and Gretel

Also known as "Hansel and Grettel", "Hansel and Grethel" or "Little brother and Little Sister", this well-known fairy tale was written by the Brothers Grimm and first published in 1812.

In a small clearing of a great forest, a woodcutter lived with his wife and their two children, Hansel and Gretel. The woodcutter was a kind but cowardly man, and although he knew that his wife was cruel to their two children, he chose to turn a blind eye. Though the woodcutter and his wife were well off, Hansel and Gretel's mother would dress them in rags and feed them only scraps left over from meals.

However, it just so happened that, one year, a great poverty spread across the land. The woodcutter and his wife became very poor, and this brought them much unhappiness. One evening, after they had gone to bed, the woodcutter found himself unable to sleep.

"What is to become of us?" he asked his wife. She pretended to think on this a while, for she had already been thinking up a plan. Eventually, she spoke.

"We have become poorer than anyone should ever be," she said, "And we can no longer live the life befitting people such as we. Hansel and Gretel – useful as they are – prove only to drain us of the little we have. So I'll tell you what I think, husband of mine. Early tomorrow morning, we will take our children into the depths of the forest, travelling further than they have ever gone before. Once there, we will light a fire for them and give them bread to eat, but then we will return home without them."

The woodcutter recoiled in horror, for he knew deep down that his wife was not kind to their children, but this? Such a terrible act was beyond forgiveness.

"Dear wife, we cannot," he said. "We must not leave our children to fend for themselves in the forest. The wild animals, the darkness, the cold . . . they would surely perish."

The woodcutter's wife sighed deeply. "If we don't, then we shall *all* perish," she said. And despite the woodcutter's arguments, his wife persisted and soon enough the weak man agreed. The two fell into a deep sleep, knowing that the following day their troubles would be halved.

But they weren't the only two awake in the house. Hansel and Gretel also lay awake – as they were given so little food that they often couldn't sleep for hunger. Upon hearing the words of their mother and father, they both grew deeply upset. "What shall we do, sister?" asked Hansel, the worry showing on his face. Gretel was quiet at first, and walked over to the window for air, as she was feeling quite unwell at the thought of what lay ahead of them. As she stood at the window, a thought sprung into her mind. "Come with me," she told her brother, and they tiptoed outside into the moonlit night. Once outside, Hansel saw what his sister had seen from their window: the white pebbles that lay in front of their house sparkled and shone in the darkness. These pebbles could lead them back home! At once they started collecting the stones, picking up as many as they could carry.

The following morning their mother woke them early. "You must come with us to collect firewood," she said, handing them each a small piece of bread to carry and hiding her lie so well that they would have believed her wholeheartedly had they not already known the truth. They set off on their journey into the woods, and as they walked along Hansel and Gretel took it in turns to drop the small white stones along the way. At one moment during their walk, their mother noticed Gretel lingering behind them. "Why do you stop so?" she asked. "Hurry yourself along." To which Gretel replied, "I'm sorry, Mother – I thought I saw a white cat amongst the trees." At another moment, their father saw Hansel crouch down low. "What are you doing, boy?" he asked, to which Hansel replied, "I thought I saw a small bird yonder, but perhaps it was nothing."

Of course, Gretel had not seen a cat and Hansel had not seen a bird. Instead, they were carefully placing the white pebbles on the ground.

When they at last reached the clearing, so far from their home, their mother pointed at two logs. "Take rest here," she said, as their father built them a fire. We will go to chop firewood and come back for you." Hansel and Gretel tried to pay attention to the direction in which their parents walked away from them, but they were so tired from their walk that they soon fell asleep.

When they awoke, the sun had set and dusk was all around them. Gretel looked up at the sky. "We wait for the moon," she said to Hansel, and he nodded in reply, for as the moon appeared from behind a cloud, it shone its light down upon them and as it did so the white pebbles they had dropped once again sparkled and shone in the darkness – a map to show their way home. Hansel smiled at

Gretel, and she in return. They started their journey back together.

After walking all night, Hansel and Gretel sighted their home through the trees just as the sun was rising. They knocked on the door. What would their mother and father make of their return? As their mother opened the door she looked very much in shock, but she composed herself quickly and feigned relief. "My dear children!" she cried. "You have returned! Thank goodness! We tried to find you in the forest, but we lost our way. It of course was our hope that you would find your way back." She called for her husband, who rushed to the door. And when the children saw his face they knew that his relief was indeed real, for tears ran down his face as he hugged them tightly. That evening, the woodcutter made sure his children ate a real meal, not the scraps they were usually given – he gave them the food from his own plate and ate the scraps himself, such was his regret. But that very night, as he was falling asleep, his wife spoke to him quietly.

"Husband of mine," she said, "we are still as poor as ever, with not enough food to survive. The children, much as I love them, cannot stay. We must take them back into the woods in the morn." The woodcutter tried to argue, but after so many years of not using his voice, he no longer really knew how. Soon enough, his wife had persuaded him of what they must do and they fell asleep.

On this night, as with the night before, Hansel and Gretel heard their parents' conversation. Though they could easily have fallen asleep after eating such a hearty meal, they had stayed awake out of fear. Upon hearing their parents' quiet snores, they crept to the front door so that they could collect white pebbles once again. But the door was locked! Did their mother suspect something? They returned to their room and lay awake for hours until exhaustion won over and they both fell into fitful slumber.

When their mother came to wake them in the morning, they feigned sleep. She asked them to dress quickly and again prepare themselves for the long walk into the woods. As they stood outside, Hansel and Gretel looked at each other in panic – what would they do now? It was only when their mother handed them each a small piece of bread that an idea sprung to Hansel's mind. As before, they started out on their walk and as before they took it in turns to leave a trail behind them – but this time it was not stones, it was bread! The woodcutter and his wife led them deeper and deeper into the woods – much further than they had ever been before. They had to use all of the bread they'd been given, but as they reached the clearing in the woods, Hansel scattered the last few morsels on to the floor. The woodcutter built a fire as his wife stood watch. "Wait here for us while we collect wood," his wife said when the fire was lit. "Do not leave this spot until we return. It's for your own safety," she added.

Hansel and Gretel *did* wait. And they even fell asleep again, such was their exhaustion from the walk. But as the moon rose high in the sky, they awoke abruptly. It was time for them to start their journey back. But as they started looking for the crumbs, an awful realization dawned on them: the crumbs were gone. Eaten by birds, perhaps, or scattered by the winds – however it had happened, they spied no crumbs along the forest floor. They started walking, trying to retrace their steps, but soon became lost. What would become of them now?

Hansel and Gretel walked all night and all day, and even walked the next night too. But still they couldn't find their way out of the forest. Eventually, so weak from tiredness were they that they sat down at the roots of an old tree and fell asleep. When they awoke, it was to the sound of their rumbling stomachs. They both sighed with weariness. But with no choice in the matter, they carried on walking, determined to find their way. At around midday they heard birdsong so sweet that they stopped to listen. Noticing a small bird high in the trees, they decided to follow it as it flew from branch to branch. On and on they went, until finally the bird rested on the roof of a small cottage. "Oh, Gretel!" cried Hansel. "A cottage – look, a cottage, we're saved!" They rushed to the house, but as they reached the garden gate they realized that something was … different. Gretel smelled the air. Something smelled … sweet? They walked closer to the house, and Gretel reached out to touch the wall. It was made of cake! The softest cake, stuck together by glistening icing. The window ledge was made of biscuits, and the windows themselves were made of clear sugar. At once, she and Hansel started nibbling at the house, taking handfuls of cake and pulling biscuits from around the windows. They hadn't eaten for days, and now they realized just how hungry they were. But as they pushed the sweet treats into their mouths, they heard a voice.

"Who's that nibbling at my house?" it said. As quick as a flash, the front door opened and a small old lady stood before them. Hansel and Gretel were so frightened that they instantly dropped the food they were holding. The woman looked at them slyly.

"Oh! My dear children, how hungry you must be – have you travelled far?" she asked, as her hard face twisted into a smile. "What brought you here?" When Hansel and Gretel found themselves too surprised to answer, she told them, "Well, whatever it was, you're safe now. Come inside and eat some more. You can't have eaten for days."

The old woman took them both by the hand, leading them into her house and sitting them at her kitchen table. "You sit there," she said, "and I'll make you a little meal." Well, let me tell you – the meal was *not* little! Plate after plate the little old lady brought them, each one stacked with cakes and sweet treats. Hansel and Gretel were so hungry that they ate it all – every last bit. And as their eyes grew heavy, the old lady led them to a room where two soft and squidgy beds stood. That night, Hansel and Gretel fell asleep thinking that they were in some sort of heaven. But this was not to be, for the old woman who had welcomed them into her house had only pretended to be friendly. But really she was a wicked witch who had built her house out of delicious foods so that she could lure children there to eat for her dinner.

Early the next morning, before Hansel and Gretel awoke, the witch looked over them both, sleeping away so peacefully. "They will be tasty indeed," she said to herself, and she grabbed Hansel with her small bony hand and carried him to a large cage while he was still half asleep and unable to fight her off. Returning to the room, she shook Gretel harshly. "Wake up!" she cried, as Gretel wiped the sleep from her eyes, "Wake up and go to fetch water for my pot. Your brother is locked in a cage, and once I've fattened him up I shall eat him." Gretel began to cry, but quickly realized that it was no use. She had to do as the witch demanded.

So every day, Hansel was fed and fed and fed, and Gretel was ordered to fetch water and clean up after the witch.

Now, upon realizing that the little old woman was in fact a witch, Hansel and Gretel remembered something their father had told them long ago;

witches have red eyes, which means that they cannot see very well. They also have a very keen sense of smell, just like animals, so they can smell humans from a long way away. One evening, after the witch had given Hansel his meal, he noticed a small bone on the floor of the cage. At once Hansel knew what to do.

Each morning, when the witch checked on Hansel to see if he was fat enough to be eaten, she ordered him to stick out his finger. "Go on," she would say, "stick out your finger, so I can feel if you're ready for eating." Well, from that day on, whenever Hansel was given this order he would hold out the little bone instead. The witch's eyes were so bad that she could not see the bone. She thought it was Hansel's finger! "Why will you not get fat?" she shouted, such was her annoyance.

Hansel and Gretel desperately tried to find a way to escape, but while Hansel was locked in the cage, Gretel knew that she would not leave him.

However, one day, the witch decided that she had waited long enough. *The boy may not be fat enough*, she thought, *but I shall eat him anyway.* She shouted at Gretel to make the fire, and Gretel felt beside herself with fear. She did as she was told, and soon the witch's oven was roaring, with flames licking at the insides. "First I will bake some bread," said the witch, and she collected the dough from her pantry. "Why don't you check that the oven is hot enough," she said to Gretel. "You'll need to climb inside it to be sure." At once Gretel knew that the witch was planning to cook her too, but she pretended that she didn't realize. "But how might I get inside?" said Gretel innocently, "The oven is not nearly big enough."

"You silly girl," said the witch, "of course it is. Even I could fit in there." And with that, the witch opened the oven door and stood so close to it that she was almost inside. Gretel seized her chance and gave the witch the biggest push she could muster. The witch fell into the oven and cried out in shock, and Gretel secured the door with a bar. Running to Hansel, she released him from his cage and they embraced with joy. "Oh, Gretel, we're saved," cried Hansel, with tears in his eyes. They left the witch's house, never looking back, and both Hansel and Gretel went on to live long and happy lives.

Little Briar Rose

Now known as "Sleeping Beauty", "Little Briar Rose" was collected by the Brothers Grimm and published in volume one of *Children's and Household Tales* in 1812. Though the Grimm version was based on the original literary tale included in Charles Perrault's *Histoires ou Contes du Temps* Passé in 1697, the earlier version was in turn based on a story called "Sun, Moon and Talia" by Italian poet Giambattista Basile.

There was once a king and queen who very much wanted a child. Much time passed but no child was born unto them, which made them very sad. Still, they dared to hope that one day their dream would come true.

Then it so happened that one afternoon, as the queen was bathing, a frog appeared before her. "Before the year is over, your wish will be fulfilled," he told the queen, "and you shall welcome a baby girl into the world."

The frog's words came true, and the king and queen did indeed have a baby girl. For this they were filled with joy and happiness. A great celebration was arranged and relatives, friends and all acquaintances were invited to share the king and queen's happiness. As well as this, the king invited the Wise Women of the kingdom, of which there were thirteen. However, in his haste, the king only invited twelve and forgot the thirteenth wise woman.

The feast was a celebration like nothing the kingdom had ever seen before, with much merriment, dancing and singing. Before long, the

Wise Women rose and surrounded the new princess. Each wise woman bestowed upon the child a gift. They chose kindness, intelligence, curiosity, strength, resilience, determination, and so on and so forth until the time came for the twelfth wise woman to speak. But just as the twelfth wise woman opened her mouth, the thirteenth wise woman stormed into the great hall, furious that she had not been invited. The king and queen professed their apologies at their mistake, but the woman, angered by them and seeking revenge, declared:

"The princess shall indeed grow to possess all of the gifts that my sisters have bestowed upon her. But in her fifteenth year, she shall prick herself on a spindle and die!"

With this, the woman left the hall as chaos engulfed the crowds of people around her. The king and queen were terribly distraught, such was their love for the child they had waited so patiently to have. And that was when the twelfth wise woman stepped forward. She could not undo the spell of the thirteenth, she said with sadness, but perhaps she could soften it slightly so that instead of dying, the princess would be taken into a deep sleep and would be hidden from the world by a forest of thorns that would prevent entry to the castle for one hundred years and would protect the princess from harm.

The king decreed that all spindles across the land be burned immediately, such was his fear of the enchantment coming true. Years passed, and the princess grew into a fine young lady showing all of the virtues that the wise women had given her. For a while, all in the kingdom lived happily. They even forgot about the terrible prophecy the thirteenth wise woman had delivered.

But on the day of the princess's fifteenth birthday, she awoke early with a start. Instead of going down to eat breakfast with her parents, she was overcome with the desire to explore the palace. Upon doing so, she came across a staircase that she had never seen before. She climbed the stone steps, feeling the air around her become cold and unwelcoming, but on she walked until she came to a door. In the lock sat a rusty old key, and when she turned it the door creaked open heavily. There, in a small room, sat an old woman busily spinning flax at a spindle.

The princess was drawn to the object most powerfully, and she reached out her hand to touch it. As soon as she pricked her finger, the curse was fulfilled and she immediately fell into a deep sleep.

As the princess fell to the floor in a magical slumber, the curse spread across the whole kingdom, consuming all within it. The king and queen fell asleep at their breakfast table, the horses fell asleep in their stalls, the dogs fell asleep in the courtyard, the birds fell asleep in the trees. The curse spread across the land like a blanket, covering it in silence. Around the castle a terrible forest of thorns grew, so dense and dangerous that nothing could get through. The legend of the sleeping princess, so called Little Briar Rose, spread to other kingdoms and many princes tried to rescue her, however the thorns knitted together as if like fingers, and the young men became stuck in them, perishing terribly.

As the years passed, many forgot about Briar Rose and the sleeping kingdom. The thorns covered it so completely that no one even noticed that it was there. But, one hundred years later, a prince came to the country. His grandfather had told him of the legend of Briar Rose, and he sought out the forest of thorns that led to her castle. He knew that many had died making the journey, but was filled with determination. But as the prince approached the thorns, a curious thing occurred: the thorns turned into flowers and parted for him, allowing him to pass through unharmed. It had been one hundred years exactly, you see, and the spell that created the thorns was now broken. Through the kingdom the prince walked, seeing people sleeping in every place – in the walkways, at tables, even on horses who were also asleep themselves. Further and further he walked, until he came to the castle. Though he had never been there before, the prince was drawn to a staircase that contained many stone steps. Finally, he reached a door and upon opening it came to the room where Briar Rose was sleeping.

So beautiful was she that at first the prince forgot himself. Kneeling down beside her, he looked at her face, so peaceful in sleep, and leaned down to kiss her forehead. As soon as he did so, Briar Rose awoke.

They went downstairs together and saw that the kingdom was starting to wake too. The king and queen looked at one another in confusion, at first not knowing what had happened. As the prince told them of the legend of Briar Rose, they listened in amazement and decided to celebrate with the kingdom once more. And so, that evening, and one hundred years late, Briar Rose celebrated her fifteenth birthday with the prince by her side.

Morozko

Also known as "Father Frost", "Morozko" is a Russian fairy tale collected by Alexander Afanasyev and included in *Russian Fairy Tales*, published in volumes between 1855 and 1863. Andrew Lang also included a version in *The Yellow Fairy Book* in 1894.

There once lived a poor widower and his daughter, whose mother, his wife, had died after becoming very ill. As the widower felt unable to look after his daughter alone, he decided to remarry. The woman he chose also had a daughter, but while the woman was kind to her own daughter and loved her very much, she was cruel to her new stepdaughter, and took every opportunity to be unkind to her. One day, the woman decided that she would find a way to get rid of her stepdaughter. "Prepare the horse," she ordered her husband, "and take your daughter somewhere far away. When you have travelled far enough, you must leave her there," she said. "Do not return unless you have done what I've said."

The old man grieved, but knew that he wasn't strong enough to stand up to his new wife. And so, the very next day, he readied the horse and asked his daughter to ride with him. It was the middle of a terrible winter, and they travelled for some time – until the man knew that they were far enough from home – before the man asked his daughter to dismount the horse. Once she had climbed down, the cowardly man rode off as fast as his horse would allow, leaving his daughter alone in the blistering cold.

The poor girl! With snow swirling around her and a wind biting at her face and hands, she sat down on a small tree trunk, shivering terribly. But before long, she became aware of a presence. It was Morozko, the father of the frost, snow and ice.

"Are you cold, child?" he asked.

But, even though the girl felt frozen from the outside in, she remained calm. "I am quite warm, thank you, Morozko," she replied, for she had long heard tales of Morozko and knew that he despised rudeness. In truth, when Morozko had first spied the girl he intended to freeze her there and then, but upon hearing the polite way in which she spoke to him, he decided to show her mercy by bringing her a warm fleece coat. The girl wrapped it around herself with relief, and Morozko bid her goodbye.

However, it was not long before he returned. "Are you cold, child?" he asked again, to which the girl replied, "I am very warm, thank you, Morozko," for she really was now feeling much warmer than before. So pleased with her politeness was Morozko that he brought a large trunk for the girl to sit upon instead of the uncomfortable tree trunk.

A little later still, Morozko again returned to ask the girl how she was. At this point, the girl was doing very well indeed and so she politely told him so while thanking Morozko for his concern. In return for her politeness, Morozko gave the girl gold and silver, and enough jewels to fill the box on which she was sitting.

Back at the girl's house, the stepmother told her husband to go fetch the body of his child. *She has been out there long enough*, she thought. *I am certain she will have perished*. The old man rode out into the forest with much trepidation. Oh, how he regretted his decision to follow his wife's orders. But when he arrived at the spot where he had left his daughter, he was overcome with joy, for there she sat, alive and well! He lifted her upon the horse, along with all of the gifts she had been bestowed, and took her back to the house. When they arrived home, the girl's stepmother was shocked to hear about what had happened. "Go back to the forest immediately," she told her husband, "but this time take my daughter." You see, the woman was very greedy, and she wanted her daughter to be given gold and silver and jewels so that she could take them for herself. The husband tried to protest, but the woman would not hear of it, and so the husband set off again, this time with the woman's daughter on the back of his horse.

Once the girl had been left in the forest, it was not long before she started shivering uncontrollably, so cold was it in the dark woods. But it was also not long before Morozko appeared, and he looked at the girl intently.

"Are you cold, child?" he asked, which the girl thought was a particularly silly question to ask someone who was stuck in the middle of a forest. "Of course I am cold, you awful man!" she cried. "Look at my hands – they are blue with frost – and my feet are quite numb. Curse you!"

Dawn had hardly broken back at the house when the old man was awoken by his wife the following morning. Gleefully, she instructed him to collect her daughter from the forest. "And be careful with the trunk of jewels!" she called after him, as he rode away. But when the man returned much later, there was no trunk filled with jewels. To the woman's horror, instead she saw the body of her daughter, frozen stiff by the snow and ice that had engulfed her in the forest. Morozko had done his worst, and the woman knew she would live the rest of her life regretting sending her daughter into the forest to her death.

The Snow Queen: A Tale in Seven Stories

Written by Hans Christian Andersen, "The Snow Queen" was published in *New Fairy Tales* in 1844 and is thought to be one of Andersen's longest and most beloved stories.

About a Mirror and Its Fragments

There was once a horribly bad hobgoblin of the most wicked sort. In fact, he was so wicked that he was the devil himself. On this particular day, the hobgoblin was feeling very pleased because he had finished making a mirror. Now, you may not think that there could be anything strange or dangerous about a mirror, but that would not be true. For, if anyone looked upon the mirror that the devil made, instead of the good, the mirror would reflect evil and ugly things in their place. In this mirror, the most beautiful sunset would appear as a raging storm, and beautiful people would look hideous. Of course, the hobgoblin was enormously pleased with his creation. He told his followers – who were just as deceitful and wicked as he – that a miracle had come to pass, for he had created a mirror that showed how the world *really* looked. His followers scurried about with the mirror until there was not a person alive who had not looked into it and seen themselves and the world in some distorted way.

But that was not enough. They wanted to fly the mirror into the sky so that it could reflect down on as much of the world as possible. Up they flew, with the mirror upon their backs and between their arms. The higher they got, the wider it stretched, until they could hardly manage to hold it. As they flew above the clouds, the mirror started to shake so violently that it slipped from their grasp and fell to earth, where it shattered into billions of tiny pieces or perhaps even more. Had it been destroyed? Oh no – now the mirror was even more dangerous than it had been before. Its many fragments – some smaller than a grain of sand – went flying about the world, blown by an invisible wind, and flew into people's eyes. These bits of glass distorted everything these people saw, and once they had settled they could never be removed. Some pieces of the glass were made into spectacles, some to windows. A few people even experienced a splinter of glass in their hearts, which was a truly terrible thing, for their hearts slowly turned to ice over many years.

The hobgoblin watched all of this and laughed with glee.

A Little Boy and a Little Girl

Deep in the city, where it was so crowded with houses and people that very few were able to have even a garden to grow plants in, two small children lived. This little boy and little girl were not brother and sister, but they loved each other as dearly as family. Their parents lived next door to each other, and the boy and girl's bedroom windows faced each other. They were so close together that it was almost possible to step from one window to another. The boy's name was Kay and the girl's name was Gerda.

In large boxes upon their window ledges, their parents had helped them to grow vegetables. They also each had grown a beautiful rose bush, with roses that were lush and as close to perfection as any rose could be. After some time, they realized that they could place these boxes sideways, so that they reached from one window to another and looked like a wall of flowers. The rose bushes threw out long sprays that framed the windows, and pea plants hung down beneath them. The boxes were very high up, and the children knew that they were not allowed to climb about on them, but they would often sit on their window ledges and play together.

Winter, of course, put an end to this. The cold set in and the windows frosted over so that nothing could be seen through them. But they would heat copper pennies on the stove and press the hot coins against the cold, frost-coated glass until a small circle of ice had melted. This made fine peepholes, and meant that Kay and Gerda could still see each other's eyes peeping through the holes. In the summer it was so easy for them to see each other, when all they needed was to open their windows. But in winter, when the snow was whirling about outside and their windows were frozen shut, it was much harder.

One evening, when they were talking to Kay's grandmother, Kay asked about the white bees. "Do they have a queen too?" he asked. "Indeed they do," said his grandmother. "She flies in the thick of the swarm and is the biggest bee of all. She is never able to be still, and at night she flies over houses and peers into windows. The windows she has looked into freeze over in a strange fashion, as if they were covered with flowers." The children knew this to be true, for they had seen frozen patterns upon their own windows. "Could the Snow Queen get inside?" asked Gerda. "Let her try!" cried Kay. "I would melt her on the hot stove."

His grandmother simply stroked his head and told them other stories.

That evening, when Kay was ready for bed, he looked out of his little peephole in the window. Snowflakes were falling all around, swirling in spirals and flying here and there. As he watched, a snowflake that was much larger than the others landed on the corner of his flower box. Bigger and bigger it grew, until at last it took the form of a woman. Dressed in white, the woman's dress appeared to be made from millions of snowflakes that glittered in the moon's light. She was beautiful and moved with such grace, but her skin was ice and her eyes – which sparkled like stars – contained no peace or rest. The woman beckoned to the boy, as if asking him to join her, and this frightened him so. Jumping down from his ledge, he moved as far away from the window as he could.

Time passed. The snow thawed and spring arrived. The sun shone brightly, and flowers bloomed, birds made nests, windows were once again opened and the children were at last able to play outside. That summer, the roses were more beautiful than they had ever been before. Gerda had learned a song that reminded her of the flowers, so she sang it to Kay and then he sang it with her.

"As roses bloom so does my heart,
I'll find you if ever we're apart."

The children kissed the roses and turned their faces towards the sunshine. What glorious summer days those were, sitting beneath the fragrant rose bushes. Kay and Gerda were looking at a picture book of birds when the clock tower struck five.

"Oh!" said Kay. "Something just went in my eye. And I feel a pain here." He was pointing to his chest, as if something had touched his heart. Gerda looked into his eye, but of course could not see anything. "I think it's gone," said Kay, but it was not gone. As you will remember, it was a piece of the hobgoblin's mirror that had flown into Kay's eye, and another piece that had pierced his heart. Poor Kay!

Suddenly he looked at Gerda. "Why are you crying?" he asked, although she was not crying at all. "It makes you look so ugly. And these roses," he said with disgust, "that one is worm-ridden, and that one is crooked." He kicked the box and broke off both of the roses, which shocked Gerda terribly.

"Why are you doing that?" she asked, and when he saw how it upset her he broke off another rose and leapt home through his own window, leaving poor Gerda all alone.

From then on, Kay was much changed. He was unkind to Gerda, and to many of the people around him. He no longer wanted to read Gerda's picture books or listen to Grandma's stories, and he took to mimicking people. If there was anything strange or unusual about them, then Kay would copy it to make other people laugh. "What a funny boy!" some people would say, but it was not funny, it was unkind. He would even tease Gerda. As well as this, Kay became fascinated with the snow. When the next winter came, he brought his large magnifying glass outside and told Gerda to look into it. "Each one is different," he said about the snowflakes. "They are far more beautiful than flowers." That winter, Kay started playing with the bigger boys in the big square, and did not invite Gerda along. In the square, the boys would tie their sledge to the backs of the farmers' carts so that they could be pulled along in the snow. Kay thought this was great fun, and when a big white sleigh came by, Kay quickly hooked his sledge on to it. The driver was dressed in white, with a white cloak and a white cap. They drove the sleigh around the square twice, turning around to look at Kay in a friendly fashion. They even nodded at Kay as if they were old acquaintances. Every time Kay started to unfasten his sledge, the driver would nod again and Kay would forget what he was doing. Kay didn't even unfasten his sledge when they drove right through the town gate and the town became smaller and smaller behind them.

The snow began to fall so quickly that it appeared like a blanket in front of them. Kay could not see his hand when he held it before his own face. Suddenly feeling scared, he unfastened his sledge, but it was no good, it was still attached somehow and the driver in front sped up so that it felt as though they were going as fast as the wind. Kay shouted loudly, but no one heard him, such was the snow that surrounded them. The snowflakes seemed to get bigger and bigger, until some were the size of Kay's hands. All of a sudden, the snow seemed to part, as if like a curtain, and the sleigh pulling Kay drove through. When the driver got up, Kay saw that their coat and cap were in fact made of snow. The driver was a woman, tall and slender, with skin of blinding white. It was the Snow Queen.

"Are you cold?" she asked, as Kay shivered from the snow. "Then you must come beneath my coat." She let him into the sleigh next to her and wrapped her coat about his shoulders. It was so heavy that he felt as if he were sinking into a snowdrift. "Still cold?" she asked, and this time she kissed him upon his forehead. Her kiss was like an icicle, and Kay felt it right in his heart, which was already turning to ice. The cold of it made him feel like he was dying, but only for a moment. When the feeling subsided, he felt quite normal and was no longer aware of the cold. Kay dragged his sleigh behind him, and the Snow Queen kissed his forehead once more, making him forget Gerda, his mother, his grandmother and everyone else back at home. "I shan't give you any more kisses," said the queen, "or I may kiss you to death." As Kay looked up at her he was overwhelmed by her beauty and could not imagine a more wonderful face. When he had first seen her outside of his window, it had looked as though she was made of ice, but now that did not seem to be true and in Kay's eyes she was perfect. He stopped feeling afraid. They flew over the skies upon black clouds, as storms whistled and roared beneath them. They flew over forests and lakes, over land and sea. Above them, the moon shone brightly and Kay kept his eyes on it throughout that long winter's night. The next day, he slept at the feet of the Snow Queen.

The Flower Garden of the Woman Skilled in Magic

How did Gerda feel when Kay disappeared? She felt more sad than anyone. Nobody knew where Kay had gone. The boys he had been sledging with said that he had gone off with the big white sleigh, but no one could say the direction in which it travelled. Some said that Kay must have fallen into the river and perished. Many tears were shed, and little Gerda shed the most. How terribly bleak those cold winter days were.

But, in time, spring came at last. "Kay is dead," Gerda said to the sunshine when it returned. *I don't believe it*, whispered the sunshine. "Kay is dead," Gerda said to the birds. "We don't believe it," they sang in return. And, slowly, Gerda started to wonder if it really was true. One morning she decided to put on her favourite pair of shoes – a red pair so new that Kay had never seen them before – and walk down to the river. It was very early, and no one else was awake, so Gerda was able to walk all the way to the river without being seen. "Is it true that you took Kay away from us?" she asked the river when she stood before it. I will give you my red shoes if you will bring him back to us." The river rippled in a strange way, and it seemed to Gerda as if it were agreeing with her. So she took her red shoes from her feet and threw them as far as she could. They landed on the riverbank, but the waves washed them right back to her. *Perhaps I should try throwing them further*, thought Gerda, and she clambered into a boat that sat moored by the riverside so that she could lean over the side of it. Once she had done this, she threw her shoes as far as she could, but it was only then that she realized the boat was not tied up. Her movement upon it had made it drift away from the bank, and now she was too far away to jump off safely. The boat gathered speed and very quickly Gerda felt quite frightened.

As the boat continued to drift downstream, Gerda noticed that her red shoes were still bobbing in the water behind it, but they weren't close enough for Gerda to reach them. On each side of the river grew the loveliest plants and flowers that were shaded by old trees. In the distance Gerda could see rolling hills with cattle and sheep upon them. But there were no people to be seen – not one.

Perhaps the river will take me to Kay, thought Gerda, and this cheered her. She watched the flowers and the hills for hour after hour. After some time, the boat drifted towards a large cherry orchard, in which stood a little house with a thatched roof and unusual red, blue and yellow windows. Outside of it stood two statues of soldiers that were carved out of wood and had their arms raised. At first Gerda thought they were people, and so she called out to them, but of course they could not reply. As the river's current pushed the boat closer to the bank, Gerda called out, louder and louder, until an old woman came out of the house. She was using a gnarled, misshapen stick to walk on and was wearing a large sun hat with flowers painted upon it – snow drops, tiger lilies and roses too. She was the oldest woman Gerda had ever seen. The woman used her stick to pull the boat into shore, and lifted Gerda out of it. Gerda was relieved to be on land once more, but was a little afraid of this unusual woman who she did not know.

"Who are you, my dear?" said the old woman, "And how did you get here?" After Gerda had told her everything, and asked if she had seen Kay, the old woman shook her head and said that no other child had come by the house but that perhaps he might one day. "Come inside for some cherries," said the woman, "and look upon my garden. The flowers within it are more beautiful than any you have ever seen. The old woman led Gerda into her house, and locked the door behind her.

Once inside, Gerda saw that all of the windows were very high up on the walls, and through their coloured panes the sunlight was transformed into a strange mixture of colours. On a table stood a bowl of deep red cherries, and when Gerda tasted them she found them to be the most delicious fruit she had ever eaten. At once she was filled with a sense of calm and, no longer afraid, she ate the whole bowlful. While she was eating, the old woman combed Gerda's hair with a golden comb. "I have so often wished for a little girl like you," said the woman. "I am sure that you and I will get along." As the woman combed her hair, Gerda forgot all about Kay and all of the people she knew, for the old woman was skilled in magic. She was not a wicked woman, but she very much wanted to keep Gerda, and she knew that, with the help of her magic, she might be able to do this. She led Gerda to her garden, which contained every flower ever known and was always in full bloom. But before the woman revealed her garden to Gerda, she pointed her stick at each of her rosebushes and used her magic to force them back into the ground. You see, she knew that if Gerda looked upon the roses then she would be reminded of Kay and try to run away. When she finally revealed the garden, Gerda was transfixed by its beauty. Why, it looked like every known flower from every season was there, all in full bloom at the same time. Gerda played in the garden until the sun went down behind the tall cherry trees. At bedtime, the woman tucked her into a bed so soft and snug that Gerda dreamt the most wonderful dreams.

The next day, Gerda went out again to play in the sunshine. And so it continued for many days. Gerda knew every flower by heart and would talk to them often. She always had the feeling that one flower was missing, but when she thought on it she could not think which flower it might be.

One afternoon, Gerda noticed again the flowers

upon the woman's hat. She had forgotten to remove the rose from it, and upon seeing the rose painted there, Gerda looked about the garden and realized that there were no roses growing there. How sad, she thought, for roses are the most beautiful flowers of all. And, without quite knowing why, Gerda sat down upon the grass and cried. As her warm tears fell into the ground below, a rose bush sprung from the earth with blooms as full as when the old woman had made it disappear. As Gerda looked upon it, she remembered her own roses, and she remembered Kay.

"Oh, how long I have been delayed," she said aloud. "I wanted to look for Kay, but I fear I have been here much longer than I can know.

"Where is Kay?" she asked the roses. "Is he dead?"

"He isn't dead," the roses replied. "We have been down in the earth where the dead are, and Kay was not there with us." Gerda rushed around the garden asking the other flowers, but none of them could answer her question. *There is no use asking the flowers*, Gerda realized, *for they only know their own stories. But I shall return home soon and bring Kay with me*. Gerda ran to the end of the garden, and though the gate was fastened she tried and tried at the latch until it gave way and the gate flew open. Out she ran, in her bare feet, looking back three times to make sure she was not being followed. At last she could run no longer, so tired was she, and she sat down to rest. When she looked up she saw that summer had passed and autumn had arrived, but inside the garden she had never seen this, for the weather there always stayed the same. Knowing that she could not waste any more time, Gerda got up to run, but, oh! how tired she felt, and how sore her feet were. As she looked about her, everything looked cold and bleak. How dreary and grey the world seemed now.

The Prince and the Princess

Gerda walked for many miles. She walked so far that when she finally stopped to rest she almost fell asleep with exhaustion. While she caught her breath at the base of a large tree, a crow swooped down from the sky and hopped along the snow in front of her. "Caw! Caw!" he said. He could see that the girl was tired and alone, and he felt kindly towards her. "What are you doing here?" he asked Gerda and, seeing that he could be trusted, Gerda told him everything and asked if he had seen Kay. At this point, the crow nodded. "I might have!" he cawed, "I really might have!"

"Really?" asked Gerda, feeling overjoyed by the news. "Please, tell me where he is."

"If he is the person I believe him to be, then he lives at the palace with the princess," said the crow. Gerda was amazed to hear this. Could Kay really live with a princess now? She begged the crow to tell her more, and so he rested on a nearby branch and began his story.

"In the kingdom where you find yourself now, there is a princess who is uncommonly clever," he said. "Such is her intelligence that she has read many books and undertaken many studies. Not too long ago, she realized that it might be nice to fall in love. But she only wanted someone with whom she could have interesting conversations," added the crow quickly. "Someone whose intelligence matched her own. The men who stood around looking impressive simply bored her. She called her ladies-in-waiting and announced her plans to them – and they were of course very excited. News spread across the kingdom – and even further afield than that – that all eligible people were invited to the palace to meet the princess and partake in a conversation with her. From this the princess would make her decision. Well, as you might guess, many people wanted to meet the princess. Outside the palace, crowds gathered in a long line that seemed to stretch for miles. And many people spoke of their confidence and said that they would be the one to win over the princess. But when each of those people finally stood in front of her they found themselves tongue-tied. It was all they could do to simply agree with every word the princess said, and of course that was not what she was looking for."

"But what about Kay?" asked Gerda, as this had fast become a rather long story indeed. "Yes, yes," said the crow, "I was just coming to that. On the third day, a person with neither horse nor carriage strode boldly to the palace. His eyes sparkled the way yours do and he was handsome but his clothes were poor."

"That sounds like Kay!" exclaimed Gerda, and relief rushed through her.

"He had a little knapsack on his back," said the crow.

"Kay didn't have a knapsack," said Gerda, "but he

did have a sledge – could it have been a sledge that you saw?"

"Perhaps," answered the crow, for he really wasn't sure. "I was told that when he entered the palace he was not scared by the guards and he walked straight up to the princess. He was not there to court the princess, he said, but to hear her wisdom, for he was very much interested in her learnings and opinions. His intellect matched hers, and because of this they were able to have many challenging conversations and she decided to make him her husband."

"Oh, that sounds very much like Kay," said Gerda happily. "He is so very clever. I must go to the palace and find him."

"I will help in whichever ways I can," said the crow, "but I must warn you, it will be difficult for you to find a way in. Wait beside that stile and I shall fly to the palace and find a way."

Gerda sat and waited, and time passed. She almost wondered if the crow might not come back, but she felt that he was a trustworthy sort and so she continued to wait. As night started to fall, the crow indeed returned.

"My lady love is a crow who resides within the

castle grounds," he said, "and she told me of a hidden doorway that grants access to the inside. I even have the key." He placed the key on the ground next to Gerda, and she took it in her hand. Then off they set towards the palace, with the crow leading Gerda directly to the door, which was just as he had said. Oh, how her heart beat with fear as she opened the door and walked through it. As she wandered through the palace, the crow directed her to a room from which she could hear voices. *Will I find Kay behind this door?* she wondered.

Upon opening it, Gerda could see that the ceiling of the room was made of glass, with a pattern that looked like an enormous tree. At once she noticed the princess sitting at a table with her prince next to her. At first Gerda thought it must be Kay, and she called out his name, but as she moved closer she realized that the prince only resembled him slightly. He was not Kay. The princess and prince asked Gerda to explain herself, and so she told them why she was there. When she had finished, they looked to each other sadly. "You poor girl," said the princess, "how terrible it is for this to have happened." The princess decided that the very next morning they would give one of their carriages to Gerda so that she may travel in it to search for Kay. "You may sleep in the palace tonight," said the princess, "and set off as early as you please in the morning." Feeling grateful for their kindness, Gerda fell asleep that night and dreamt of Kay. In her dream, she saw him on his sledge, which was being pulled by beings that looked like angels.

The next day, the princess gave Gerda clothes and shoes, for her own had become awfully tattered, and led her out to a beautiful carriage made of pure gold. Helping her into the carriage, they wished her luck.

"Farewell! Farewell!" they called, as Gerda rode away from them. Looking up at the sky, Gerda saw the crow flying alongside her for quite some time, until it was time for him to bid her goodbye. At this point, the crow flew up into the tree and waved his graceful black wings for as long as he could still see the carriage.

The Little Robber Girl

Into the dark forest the carriage rolled, deeper and deeper. As sunlight shone through the trees, it reflected on the gold of the carriage and caught the eyes of some robbers who were walking nearby. "That carriage is made of gold!" they cried, "we must steal it for ourselves." They stood in front of the carriage and pulled Gerda from it. "Look at her expensive clothes!" one of them said, eyeing up the clothes the princess and prince had given Gerda. A robber woman thought they should kill Gerda and steal everything from her, but the woman's daughter, a little robber girl who was quite wild, did not like this idea. "She must play with me," said the robber girl. "She must give me her fancy clothes and the shoes upon her feet, and she must play with me." The robber girl declared that she wanted to ride in the carriage, and because she was spoiled her mother agreed, and the robber girl and Gerda climbed into the carriage. Away they drove, further into the forest. The girl was no taller than Gerda but was obviously much stronger. She put her arms around Gerda protectively. "They won't kill you unless I get angry with you," she said. "And I think you're a princess." Gerda explained that she was not a princess, but that she had met one and she once again told the story of how she came to find herself there. When she had finished, the robber girl looked at her gravely and dried her eyes.

The carriage stopped at last, and when Gerda looked outside she saw that they were in the courtyard of the robbers' castle. Crows and ravens flew about the roofs and the walls were cracked from bottom to top. It was an ominous looking place. The robber girl led her to an enormous hall where a big fire was burning. "Tonight, you will sleep here with me and my little animals," said the girl, and in the corner of the hall Gerda saw that beds were made up from straw and blankets. On perches around the bed sat nearly a hundred pigeons. "They are all mine," said the robber girl, following Gerda's gaze. There was a reindeer too, which the robber girl had named Bae. Gerda noticed that, though the girl claimed to love the animals, she kept them all imprisoned in the hall and treated them coarsely. "Tell me your story again," demanded the girl, and so Gerda obliged. As she spoke, the pigeons listened and watched. When the girl was tired, she demanded that Gerda lie next to her so that she could be sure of her not running away. The girl fell asleep and began snoring loudly, but Gerda couldn't possibly sleep, so overcome was she by fear. She didn't know if she would live or die.

Presently, a pigeon came to rest beside her. "Coo," it said. "Coo, coo. We have seen your Kay. He was sat in the Snow Queen's sleigh; they swooped over the trees when we were in our nest and the Snow Queen blew upon my family so that they would die. I was able to escape."

"Do you know where the Snow Queen was going?" asked Gerda. To which the pigeon replied, "She was bound for Lapland, the land of snow and ice. Just ask the reindeer who stands beside you."

Gerda did indeed ask the reindeer, who said that the pigeon was telling the truth. "Oh, Kay, I hope that you are safe," sighed Gerda, and she fell into a fitful sleep.

In the morning, Gerda told the robber girl all that the pigeons had told her. The robber girl was quiet for a while, but then got up and walked over to the reindeer. "Do you know where Lapland is?" she asked, and of course the reindeer did, for he was born there. The robber girl decided to let the reindeer go as long as he agreed to carry Gerda to the Snow Queen's palace in Lapland. The reindeer was enormously pleased to be granted his freedom back in return for this one task.

After hoisting Gerda on to the reindeer's back, the robber girl distracted her mother and the other robbers so that they could escape. She had given Gerda warm gloves to wear and two loaves of bread to eat. With these provisions secured to the back of the reindeer, Gerda set off. "Goodbye," she said quietly, waving behind her to the robber girl. Over stumps and stones the reindeer bounded, through the trees and snow. Wolves howled and ravens shrieked, but on they went until finally Gerda could see bright colours streaking the sky far ahead of them. "Those are the Northern Lights," said the reindeer. "I'm almost home," and he ran even faster than he had before. They travelled night and day, and by the time the loaves of bread were eaten they found themselves in Lapland.

The Lapp Woman and the Finn Woman

After the reindeer had been running for quite some time, they stopped in front of a small dwelling that had a roof so low it almost touched the ground. The doorway was low too – such was it that anyone coming in or out of it had to lie on their stomach to do so. A Lapp woman lived there and, at the moment when Gerda and the reindeer stopped by, she was cooking fish over an oil lamp. The reindeer told her his story, and Gerda's too, which he realized was much more important. Gerda was so cold that she struggled to say a thing. "Oh, you poor creatures," said the woman, "What a terribly long journey. And you still have such a long way to go, for you will need to travel hundreds of miles into Finmark. That is where the Snow Queen currently resides. I will write you a message that you must take to the Finn woman who lives near there. She will be able to tell you more about the Snow Queen than I."

As soon as Gerda had warmed up and had something to eat and drink, the Lapp woman handed her a dried codfish on which she had written the message for the Finn woman because she didn't own any paper. Gerda and the reindeer readied themselves to travel again, and waved goodbye to the Lapp woman. Off the reindeer ran, with Gerda strapped securely to his back. The skies were bursting with colours as the Northern Lights flashed above their heads.

At last they came to Finmark and found the residence of the Finn woman. They knocked on her chimney, for they could not locate a door. Once inside, they found that it was extremely hot. Gerda struggled to take off her mittens and boots quickly enough and needed to loosen her clothes. The Finn woman put a piece of ice on the reindeer's head to keep him cool, and read the message on the codfish three times so that she knew it by heart. Once she was confident that she did, she put the fish into a kettle of soup, for she never wasted anything and thought that they could eat it later on.

After listening to their stories, the woman did not have anything to say, but in her silence the reindeer saw much wisdom. "You are a wise woman," he said to her separately, "won't you give this girl something that will help her face the Snow Queen? Is there not a potion that will make her as strong as twelve men?"

But the woman just sniffed. "Twelve strong men?" she said. "Much good that would be." But the woman could see how desperate the reindeer was to help Gerda, and so she shared with him some of her deepest wisdom. "I cannot give any power as great as the power she already has," the woman explained. "Don't you see how all are compelled to serve her – and how far she has come in this world? Strength lies within her heart because she is a sweet, innocent child. And if she herself cannot reach the Snow Queen and rid her dear friend Kay of the shards of glass that we know afflict him, then there is no help we can give her. The Snow Queen's garden lies around eight miles from here," the woman continued. "Carry the girl there and put her down by the large bush covered with red berries. Once you have done so, hurry back here."

It was time once again for Gerda and the reindeer to move on. The Finn woman's house was so hot inside that Gerda forgot to put on her boots and mittens, only realizing her mistake when they were back outside and on their way. How quickly she felt the cold on her skin, and though she gasped with the shock of it, the reindeer dared not stop. It was only when he came to the bush with the red berries that the reindeer set Gerda down and said goodbye with tears coming down his face. Then off he ran, back the way he came, leaving Gerda without boots and without mittens, right in the middle of icy Finmark.

Snowflakes blew around Gerda, and as she grew closer to the Snow Queen's garden, the snowflakes grew bigger and bigger. Gerda remembered how large the flakes had looked underneath Kay's magnifying glass, but here they were far larger and imposing, for they were the Snow Queen's guard and the shapes they took were most strange. Some looked like overgrown porcupines, some were like a large knot of snakes struggling to be free, with heads and tails protruding in every direction. Others looked like fearsome bears. But all of them were a glistening white, for they were of course made of snow. It had become so cold that Gerda could see her breath freezing in front of her mouth in clouds. Thicker and thicker the clouds of breath appeared, and bigger and bigger they became, until they took the shape of little angels carrying shields and lances. They struck the snowflake creatures ahead of Gerda, protecting her from them so that Gerda may walk on undisturbed. And so she did, walking right up to the Snow Queen's palace.

What Happened at the Snow Queen's Palace, and What Came of It

The walls of the Snow Queen's palace were made entirely of snow that had built up over many years to become strong and impenetrable. The windows and doors were made of thick sheets of ice, and the many rooms and corridors stretched for about a mile, each one lit by the Northern Lights that flared above them. In the middle of the palace stood a large frozen lake that was cracked into a thousand pieces, each piece shaped exactly the same as the next. The lake looked like it had been created by a wonderful craftsperson. In the centre of the lake stood the Snow Queen's throne. She called the lake her Mirror of Reason, and felt it was the most beautiful thing in the world. It happened that, at this time, the Snow Queen was absent from the palace, but one person did remain there: Kay. His skin was blue from cold, but Kay did not feel it, so under the Snow Queen's spell was he. His heart had now almost completely turned to ice.

Distractedly, Kay was moving pieces of ice to and fro, trying to fit them into every possible pattern as if they were a puzzle. To him, what he was doing seemed remarkable and highly important, for the glass in his eye and heart made him believe it. But no matter how he moved the pieces, Kay never felt satisfied.

Gerda had made her way through the hallways and through many rooms, and had not seen but one person on her way, so when she came across what seemed to be the last door in the palace, she felt nervous indeed. Pushing it open, she saw a beautiful frozen lake ahead of her, and noticed a boy sitting to the side of it. With a gasp, she realized the boy was Kay. She recognized him straight away, though he was much changed. At once she ran to him and embraced him warmly. "My dearest Kay," she said, "I've found you at last." But instead of seeing her, Kay sat very still. He was as cold as ice, and as stiff as a board. Holding his face in her hands, she demanded that he recognize her. "It's me," she said. "It's *me* – Gerda." When she at last realized that it was no use, she wept with sadness, and once again pulled Kay toward her in an embrace. As tears ran down Gerda's face, they fell on to Kay and went straight to his heart, melting the ice that had been consuming it and ridding it of the shard that had pierced it. And as she wept, Gerda sang:

"As roses bloom so does my heart,
I'll find you if ever we're apart."

Without knowing why, Kay started to cry – just

one tear at first, but once that had fallen it was as if floodgates had opened. He cried so freely that the piece of glass that had for so long been lodged in his eye was washed out. Stumbling back in surprise, Kay looked at the person in front of him and recognized her immediately. "Gerda!" he cried, and they clung to each other in happiness. Hand in hand, Gerda and Kay walked out of the Snow Queen's palace, safe in the knowledge that they would never go back. For, once a heart has been touched so purely by love, it can never again be claimed by ice.

Rumpelstiltskin

While the story of Rumpelstiltskin may have originated around 4,000 years ago, it was the Brothers Grimm version, "Rumpelstilzchen", that first gained widespread popularity.

Once upon a time there was an old miller and his daughter. The miller was a very poor man indeed but his daughter didn't want for much, happy was she with the little they had.

One day, the miller heard that the king would be visiting the town in which they lived. Oh, how excited he was at the thought of meeting a real-life king! The day soon arrived, and as the king passed by in his procession, he dismounted to talk to his loyal subjects. He even spoke to the miller! But as the king politely asked after the miller's life and family, the miller suddenly felt ashamed. What would a wise and wealthy king think of him, a poor miller who had no riches in the world? Trying his best to impress the king, the miller chose to lie to him.

"I have a daughter who can spin straw into gold!" he said, much to the king's surprise.

As you can imagine, the king was very interested in this revelation, in fact, he ordered the miller to bring his daughter to the palace at once so that she may spin straw into gold for him. The miller was dismayed – now he would not only lose his daughter, but also be discovered as a liar.

With much sadness, the miller's daughter accepted her fate and went with her father to the palace, where they were promptly separated without so much as a goodbye. The young woman was led to a large room filled almost completely with straw – the only space left was for a spindle that sat in one of the corners.

"Spin all of this straw into gold," the king told the woman. "If you do not, I shall be forced to punish you for your father's deceit." And with that, he left the room and locked a big iron door behind him.

The woman stood for a moment, staring at the straw. She couldn't spin this straw into gold – not even one piece of it, let alone all of it! Feeling sure that she would be sentenced to death in the morning, she fell to the floor and started to cry.

After a short while, a very small man with peculiar features spoke to her as if from nowhere.

"Why are you crying so, young lady?" he asked.

The woman looked about the room in surprise. The door was still locked. Where had this curious man come from? "The king has ordered me to spin all of this straw into gold," said the woman after she had composed herself, "but I do not know how to do that and I fear that I shall die tomorrow as a result."

The little man looked at her with his sly eyes. "What will you give me if I spin the straw into gold?" he asked. The woman didn't have much, but she instantly felt for the necklace that hung around her neck. "I shall give you this," she replied. To her surprise, without another word the man sat down at the spindle and began his work. Before her very eyes, he was spinning the straw into gold!

At sunrise, the woman heard a key turning in the lock of the giant door that imprisoned her, and she knew that the king had come to claim his treasure. When he observed the room full of glistening gold thread, he was pleased beyond measure. But instead of allowing her to leave, he asked another task of her. Taking her to an even *larger* room, the king pointed to an even *larger* pile of straw. "Tonight you must spin *this* into gold," he said. "Please, do as I say if you value your life."

As before, the woman was locked in the room with no means for escape, and as before she so feared for her life that she was reduced to tears. But, also as before, the little man silently appeared.

"What will you give me if I spin all of *this* straw to gold?" he asked her, to which she replied, "The ring from my finger," for it was the only belonging in the world that she now possessed. The little man took it gladly and set to work at the spindle.

The following morning when the king entered the room, he was amazed to see even more gold thread filling the room. So pleased was he that he clapped his hands together with joy. But instead of allowing the woman to leave, he took her to an even *larger* room with even *more* straw within it. "Tonight you must spin every last strand of this straw into gold," he said, turning to her. "And if you succeed, you shall become my wife."

When she was alone once more, the woman sat amongst the straw in silence. If she became the queen then her life would be spared, but if the king came back in the morning and there was no gold then she would surely be sentenced to death. She waited to see if the strange little man would visit her again, and in time he did. "What will you give me if I spin the straw into gold this time?" he asked. But the woman had already bestowed upon him her necklace and ring. "I have nothing left to give," she said with sadness. The man looked at her from the corner of his eye. "There may be another way," he said. "When you are queen, you must give me your first child." The woman drew her hand to her mouth in horror, but then... *I will not bear a child for quite some time*, she thought, *and who knows where this little man will be then. Perhaps I should agree to his demand.* And so she did. When morning came and the king looked upon all of the gold in the room, he proposed to the woman at once.

Some time later, the king and queen welcomed a wonderful baby girl into the world. The queen had not thought of the deal she had made with the little man for a long time; in fact, she had not thought of the little man at all. And so it was with great sadness that she saw him come to visit her the night of her baby girl being born.

"Now that you are with child, you must give her to me," said the man. "After all, we made a deal." The queen was deeply upset, and so furious with herself for agreeing to such a deal in the first place. She begged the man to take something else – *anything* else – and offered him all the gold in the kingdom if he would leave without her precious child. But the man said no. After the queen had been begging for some time, the man decided to play a cruel game on her. "Very well," he said. "If you can guess my name then I shall let you keep your daughter. I will allow you three days!"

Grateful for the chance, the queen accepted, and once the little man had disappeared she stayed up all night thinking of names.

When the little man returned on the first night, the queen read out a long list of names – all of the names she knew. The man sat there with a terrible smile on his face. "That is not my name," he said every time, taking great satisfaction in the queen's failing. The next day, the queen sent a messenger into the town and into the country in the hope that they would discover the awful man's name. One of the messengers returned with a long list of names, and when the man returned that night, the queen read them all out to him. But again, the man smiled at her cruelly. "That is not my name," he said each time. And when the queen had run out of names, the man disappeared.

The morning of the final day arrived, and the queen felt deeply unhappy. She did not know the little man's name, and she had completely run out of ideas. But then one of her messengers returned and told her a story.

"I have not been able to find any new names for you," he said, "but a most curious thing happened when I was travelling through the woods in the very early hours of this morning. I spotted a fire burning brightly in front of a small dwelling, and thought to stop awhile and warm myself, but as I got closer I realized that a strange little man was dancing around it singing songs. As I listened carefully, I heard his words:

"Some may call me small and wild,
but I shall get the poor queen's child.
She only has herself to blame,
for Rumpelstiltskin is my name!"

Upon hearing this, the queen was filled with relief. The messenger left her and she waited for the little man to appear. Soon enough, there he was. "So, dear Queen, what is my name?" he asked with glee. The queen pretended to consider his question.

"Is your name Kaspar?" she asked. "Is it Balzer?"

"No and no!" he shouted.

"Is it Melchoir? Kunz? Heinz?" asked the queen.

"No, no, NO!" shouted the man, growing louder and louder.

The queen paused. "In that case," she said, "could your name be … Rumpelstiltskin?"

The little man's eyes went wide and his face turned red. "Who told you?" he demanded. "WHO TOLD YOU?" But the queen would not say. In his anger, Rumpelstiltskin stamped and stamped and stamped his feet so hard that he fell through the stone floor. The queen never ever saw him again.

King Midas and the Golden Touch

The story of King Midas is one of the most popular Greek myths of all, telling a cautionary tale of greed. Some historical records suggest that the character of King Midas was based on a real-life king who may have lived in the seventh or eighth centuries.

There was once a king named Midas, who ruled over a prosperous and peaceful land. King Midas was extremely wealthy, and lived in a lavish palace with his daughter, Marigold, who was kind, generous, and loved by all in the kingdom, especially the king himself.

One day, as King Midas and Marigold were walking through the palace gardens, they heard a faint voice calling for help. As they hurried towards the voice, they saw a satyr lying at the entrance to the palace. Half-man and half-goat, satyrs were rarely seen this far from the forest.

"May I have some water?" said the satyr. "I have been travelling for days but lost my way."

The king, so distressed was he that the satyr was unwell, called for water immediately and at once decided that the satyr would stay at the palace until he had returned to health.

That evening, and every evening for a week, the satyr feasted with the king and his daughter. Once his strength had returned, the satyr travelled back to his homeland with the king as his escort.

On their arrival, King Midas realized that the satyr was a student of the god Dionysus, who was much relieved to see him safe. To thank Midas for his act of kindness, Dionysus offered to grant him one wish.

"I wish for whatever I touch to turn to gold," said Midas, without hesitation.

Dionysus paused for a moment. "Are you sure?" he asked. "A wish such as this one must not be made lightly." But King Midas was certain, and upon seeing this, Dionysus clapped his hands together, making an almighty sound. Suddenly it was morning and King Midas was back at his palace, wondering if it had all been a dream.

Nervously, he reached out to touch the table that stood beside his bed. As soon as he did, it turned to gold. Real gold! Why, King Midas was elated! He ran down to the breakfast room and picked up a cup to drink from, smiling with delight when the cup turned to gold. But his smile soon faded when he realized that the water inside the cup had *also* turned to gold. Midas quickly grabbed the jug itself, hoping to pour more water but, as soon as he did so, the jug and its contents sparkled and glistened; they too were now gold. He stood before the table with increasing panic and looked upon the foods piled on to plates in front of him. Time after time he grasped for the food and time after time it turned to gold beneath his fingers before, finally, there was no food left before him.

As his daughter Marigold rushed into the room for her breakfast, King Midas called out to her, so deep was his despair. Marigold reached out to comfort him, and he stretched out his hand to feel her touch. But even as the very tips of his fingers brushed hers he realized what he had done. Within the blink of an eye, Marigold was no longer his living, breathing daughter, but instead stood before him as if a gold statue.

The king wept bitterly as he understood the price he now had to pay for his awful greed. He was the king with the golden touch, but he had taken his blessings for granted and learned too late what was truly valuable to him.

Ali Baba and the Forty Thieves

The story of Ali Baba is thought to have originated in Aleppo, in modern-day Syria. It was popularized by Antoine Galland in his translated version of *The Thousand and One Nights*, which published in twelve volumes between 1704 and 1717 and contains the earliest-known written version of the tale.

Many years ago, in a town in Persia, lived two brothers called Cassim and Ali Baba. Upon their father's death, inheritance was split between them, and for a while they both lived prosperously. However, after some time they had spent all of their money and they both found themselves to be quite poor. Cassim fell in love with a wealthy woman, and so began to live a rich life. But Ali Baba fell in love with a poor woman, and so lived modestly.

One day, when Ali Baba was cutting wood in the forest, he heard the stomp of horse hooves and the call of men and women. Fearing bandits, he hid silently in a nearby bush and awaited their approach. As they came nearer, Ali Baba saw that the group totalled forty, and each one looked as fearsome as the next. They pulled up their horses right at the spot where Ali Baba hid, and at first he thought that they had seen him, but instead of coming into the bushes, one man, who Ali Baba assumed to be their captain, approached a large rock protruding from a very steep hill.

"Open, sesame!" he called out, standing before it,

and Ali Baba was amazed to see the rock roll to one side all by itself, thus revealing an entrance. One by one, the forty people walked through. *It must be very large inside*, thought Ali Baba, *if forty people are able to stand within it all at the same time*. He decided to lie in wait until the thieves had gone, and so sat down on the ground, still hidden by the bushes. Much time passed, and Ali Baba started to feel quite uncomfortable, sitting as he was beneath the shrub. But finally the thieves emerged from the rock face, one by one. When at last their captain emerged too, he stood in front of the entrance and called out, "Close, sesame!" With this, the rock rolled back into place, hiding the entrance once more. Within moments the men and women were back on their horses and riding through the woods the way they had come.

Ali Baba watched them ride away for as long as his eyes could see them. Only when he at last felt sure that the thieves were not coming back did he dare to approach the rock himself. Remembering the words he had heard the captain speak, Ali Baba called out, "Open, sesame!" Just as before, the rock moved itself to reveal the entrance behind it. Cautiously, Ali Baba walked through the opening. Inside, he was surprised to see that the cave was brightly lit – though *where* exactly the light was coming from, he could not tell, as there were no windows that he could see. But that was not the most exciting thing that Ali Baba saw, for as large as the room he now found himself in was – and it did appear to stretch for miles – he saw that it was entirely filled with treasures! There were large bales of silk, and luxurious carpets rolled up and piled high, great gold plates of all sizes sitting alongside gold statues, and bags and bags of gold coins. In fact, there were so many gold coins that bags of them piled up above Ali Baba's head. For a moment he was rooted to the spot in amazement, but, when his wits returned, Ali Baba knew that he must not stay in this place long, for the thieves might return. Quickly, he filled his sack to the brim with gold coins, and when he was once more back outside, he said, "Close, sesame!" and the rock moved back into place.

Once Ali Baba was home, he rushed to tell his wife all that he had seen. She was worried about the danger he had been in, but also grateful that he had been able to bring back gold for them. "How much gold is there, I wonder?" she said, to which Ali Baba did not know the answer. So she made a visit to her sister-in-law, to borrow scales for weighing. Before she did, Ali Baba gave her a warning. "Do not tell them of the gold," he said, "for this secret must be ours and ours alone." His wife promised to keep the secret. When she arrived at her sister-in-law's, she found many questions awaited her. "What is it you would like to weigh?" asked her sister-in-law, as she thought that Ali Baba and his wife were still very poor. "Just some grain that we hope to sell," replied Ali Baba's wife, but her sister-in-law was suspicious. As a test, she discretely put some wax in the bottom of the scale, so that it would catch some of whatever was put inside. Unknowingly, Ali Baba's wife thanked her gratefully. Once at home, Ali Baba and his wife measured the gold coins carefully and were much pleased with the amount. This would help them to live comfortably! But when Ali Baba returned the scales to his sister-in-law, he failed to realize that a gold coin was still inside, stuck to the wax. This time his brother, Cassim, was at home, and because Cassim's wife had already told him of her suspicions, he looked straight into the scales and found a gold coin so ancient that he could not tell when it was made. "I believe you keep secrets from me, brother," said Cassim, for as far as he knew, his brother was poor, but now he could see that this was no longer the case. Ali Baba tried to keep his brother's questions at bay, but it was no use. Eventually he told him all about the cave filled with riches. Upon hearing this, Cassim demanded that Ali Baba tell him the exact words needed to open the cave and where he could find it. Though Ali Baba warned Cassim of the dangers, he would not listen and decided that he would set off to the cave as soon as the sun started to rise the next day.

As planned, Cassim set off early in the morning, and soon enough he came across the place where he believed the riches to be hidden. Standing before the rock, he called out, "Open, sesame!" As the rock rolled to one side to allow him entrance, he rubbed his hands together mischievously. To and fro he walked, filling sacks with treasures and dragging them to the entrance of the cavern. But on his last trip back to his increasing stash, he saw with a shock that he had stayed within the cave for so long that the door had sealed shut behind him without warning. In his surprise, he struggled to recall the words he needed to command the entrance. "Open, barley!" he cried in panic, but of course the rock did not move. Cassim had not expected anything like this to happen and thus was ill prepared, soon realizing that all he could really do was hide and wait for the thieves to return, and then try to escape. So this is what he did. When he finally heard the thundering of horses hooves and the calls of men and women, he knew the thieves were close. In that moment, Cassim decided that as soon as the door was opened, he would run for his life. In time he saw that the rock was moving to allow the thieves entrance. He readied himself. But as he went to run through the entrance that emerged, Cassim only ran straight into the thieves, who caught him immediately. Seeing the bags that Cassim had intended to steal, the thieves ended his life immediately. To deter any other person from entering the cave, the thieves cut Cassim into four pieces and hung those pieces inside the entrance of the cave.

That night, when Cassim didn't come home, his wife grew more and more worried. Where could he be? Had he run into danger? Feeling desperate, she ran to Ali Baba and his wife. At first, Ali Baba tried to reassure her, but then his own wife spoke to him. "Your brother could be in real danger," she said with concern, and Ali Baba knew that he must go back to the cave. Travelling under the cover of night, Ali Baba worried for his brother. And as he approached the cave, he spotted his brother's donkey still roped to a tree. Suddenly he started to fear the worst. As he uttered the magic words and walked through the mouth of the cave, Ali Baba was dismayed to see the four pieces of his brother that hung inside. Grief-stricken, he fell to his knees and wept. But he knew that he could not stay there long, for it was far too dangerous. Putting his brother's remains into sacks, Ali Baba took the body back to his brother's home.

When he knocked on the door, his brother's maid Morgiana answered. Her presence was a relief to Ali Baba, as he knew Morgiana to be both intelligent and quick thinking. After telling her the occurrences of the past few days, Ali Baba implored Morgiana to help him. "My brother must be buried with dignity. No one can know that his death was unnatural – if the thieves find out who he was, they will surely come for me too. Please, tell Cassim's wife what has happened," he continued, before finally asking Morgiana to help him place the body in Cassim's house. That night, as Ali Baba fell asleep wishing he had never found out about the secret cave, Morgiana stayed up late thinking about how they could cover up the terrible way Cassim had met his end.

Early the next morning, Morgiana went straight to the local healers. In deceit, she told them that Cassim was severely ill – did they have medicine for an illness such as his? After pressing her for more information, they gave her medicine and urged her to let them know if the situation got worse. Convinced that they had believed her lie, Morgiana bid them goodbye. That day, upon Morgiana's instruction, Ali Baba and his wife made a great show of visiting their brother's house and talking to people about his deteriorating health. News soon spread that Cassim was extremely unwell. It looked like Morgiana's plan was working. That evening, she went back to the healers. "I fear nothing will help Cassim now," she said through pretend tears, "but please, give me something to assist him in his final moments." After leaving the healers, Morgiana visited an old cobbler who she knew had not been acquainted with Cassim. "Baba Mustapha," she implored, as she pushed a gold coin into his hands. "I urgently need your assistance, but I must warn you, I need to lead you somewhere blindfolded." Baba Mustapha hesitated at her words. "Do you wish me to do something against my conscience?" he asked, "and against my honour?" But Morgiana tried to persuade him otherwise. Pushing another gold coin into his hands, she pressed the matter. "Please," she said, "come with me and fear nothing. I only ask for your help as a master embroiderer." This piqued Baba Mustapha's interest and he agreed to go with her. Binding his eyes with a handkerchief, Morgiana led Baba Mustapha back to Cassim's residence, where the pieces of his body now lay. Standing Baba Mustapha before the pieces, Morgiana finally loosened his blindfold. Baba Mustapha exclaimed in horror at what he saw, and at first could not understand why she had brought him there. But Morgiana explained; she wished him to sew Cassim's body back together. Finally Baba Mustapha agreed, and Morgiana left him to work after pressing one more piece of gold into his hands.

After Baba Mustapha had finished his task, Morgiana blindfolded him once more and led him away from the residence. Leading him back, she made him promise not to tell a soul about what he had done. Once he had agreed, she quickly left before he could remove his blindfold and see the direction in which she had fled.

On her return, Morgiana prepared Cassim's body for burial, and shortly after that she spread the news that Cassim had died – of course omitting the true circumstances of his death. Ali Baba and his wife moved into Cassim's home so that they could help support his wife, and so, because of their deceit, nobody had even the smallest suspicion of what had really happened to Cassim.

It was while these events unfolded that the forty thieves returned to their cave and found with surprise that the body they had left there as a warning had since been moved. "This plainly shows that someone else knows about this place and how to gain access to it," said the captain. "For our own sake, we must find them and sentence them to death." One by one, some of the thieves stepped forward to proclaim that they would be the one to uncover the identity of this person. The search for Ali Baba thus began. One thief in particular set about talking to the townsfolk to gain information. For days on end he spoke to people on street stalls and in shops, but he did not hear anything of value until he joined in conversation with Baba Mustapha. It was early one morning, before many people had woken, and Baba Mustapha was already hard at work. "Good morning to you," said the thief, "you must be an honest man indeed if you start work at such an early hour. But how is it that a man of your age can see so well before the sun has fully risen?" Baba Mustapha was flattered by the thief, and easily lulled into a false sense of trust. His eyesight was so extraordinary, he explained, that he had in fact sewn together the pieces of a dead man in much less light. "A dead man?" exclaimed the thief, pretending to show surprise. "Oh indeed," said Baba Mustapha. "But I was sworn to secrecy, so you must not speak of this to anyone else." "I will ask you no further questions except for this," said the thief, "in which house did the dead body lie when you performed your task?" He was sure he was about to learn the exact information he was looking for, and it was all he could do to remain calm. But Baba Mustapha's reply disappointed the thief terribly. "If I knew that information, I would surely share it with you," Baba Mustapha said, "but I surely do not. You see, I walked the whole way blindfolded." The thief thought on this for a while before an idea occurred to him. "Perhaps you would remember the way if you were blindfolded once more," he suggested, and Baba Mustapha agreed, for as well as being a convincing man the thief had also offered him three gold coins for his troubles. At once the thief applied the blindfold and Baba Mustapha started to recall his journey. Walking along the cobbled pathways, the thief paid great attention to his surroundings so as not to forget. After a short while, they arrived at their destination. "It was here," announced Baba Mustapha confidently, and he pulled off the blindfold. Thanking him for his time, the thief remained outside the house as Baba Mustapha took leave. While no one was looking, the thief marked the front door with chalk and took leave himself. He would come back under the cover of night and exact his revenge then, he decided.

Not long after the thief had departed, Morgiana made to leave the house for her morning tasks, but upon opening the door she immediately saw the chalk mark. *For what purpose is this here?* she wondered to herself, quickly deciding that no good could come of the mark's presence. Noting that no other house showed a mark on its door, Morgiana set to work: collecting a piece of chalk from inside, she visited each nearby house and made a chalk mark on the door, taking great care to make sure that each mark looked identical.

That day, the thief returned to his comrades and shared with them the story he had been told. "I now know where he lived," he said with satisfaction, "and when I go back there tonight whoever still lives under that roof will live no more."

That night, the thief returned to the place where Ali Baba and his wife now lived with Cassim's wife and Morgiana. He brought a number of men and women with him. But as they approached the houses they saw that each one bore a chalk mark on its door, and the thief who had made the mark could not remember which door he had first drawn the mark upon. Realizing that their plan had been foiled, they were forced to return to their hideout. Upon doing so, another of the thieves decided to visit Baba Mustapha to find out which house he had gone to. This was done easily, for Baba Mustapha found flattery in the thief's words and quickly agreed to be blindfolded once more. Once the thief had determined the house's location, she marked the door with chalk once more, but this time the chalk was red and the thief made the marking in a much more discreet way so that it was hardly noticeable. However, the thief had not realized how keen Morgiana's eyes were, for even though the mark was small and well-hidden, she still noticed it, and when the thief returned that night with a small band of men and women, they were once again thrown into confusion. For each house bore exactly the same mark as the next.

When they returned defeated for a second time, the captain decided to take matters into his own hands. When he visited Baba Mustapha, he flattered the man just as the others had before, and blindfolded him just as he had been before. But instead of relying on a mark to identify the house, the captain paid close attention to his surroundings so that he would remember the house whether it was marked or not. Once he was sure of this, he travelled back to the cave and addressed the thieves who followed him. "There is a man who knows how to gain access to this cave," he shouted. "He will pay for this knowledge with his life. Now that I know where he lives, we shall knock on his door in plain sight and pretend to be travellers stuck in place for the day and night. I will ask to store a number of oil barrels on his premises. But inside the barrels you will hide, and when the moment comes you can leap from the barrels so that we may exact our revenge upon him and his family." Not knowing the fate that awaited them, Ali Baba slept soundly that night.

The following day, the captain's plan unfolded just as he had hoped. Upon knocking at Ali Baba's door, he found the man to be welcoming and hospitable. Ali Baba readily agreed to let the captain stay on his premises and for the barrels to be stored in his yard – he even helped move some of the barrels himself. That night, Ali Baba dined with his guest and asked Morgiana to prepare a room so that their guest would have a comfortable stay. This Morgiana did, but as she readied a lamp for their guest, she realized that their own stock of oil was all but depleted. Thinking quickly, Morgiana resolved to use some oil from one of the barrels, as surely their guest would not mind them using the oil for his own benefit?

On approaching one of the barrels, Morgiana rested a container upon its top, making a small tapping noise as she did so. As she was about to lift the barrel's lid, she was much surprised to hear a voice come from within it. "Is it time?" the voice asked, in quiet whisper. Though Morgiana felt alarm, she also knew that she could not show it. "Not yet," she replied. "Not yet, but presently." This exchange was repeated 39 times, as Morgiana knocked on each barrel. By this means, Morgiana established that there were thirty-nine men and women hiding in the barrels. Including the man, who Morgiana now assumed to be their leader, the count totalled forty. Straight away, Morgiana set to work boiling pot after pot of water. Once boiled, she poured it into the barrels one at a time, stifling the sounds within by keeping the lids fastened securely. In this way, every one of the thirty-nine thieves perished painfully. Once her task had been completed, Morgiana took up a hiding place, lying in wait for the captain to emerge. In due course this happened, and the leader of the thieves snuck out to the yard with the view to release each man and woman from their barrel. But upon doing so, the captain was horrified to find only scorched remains within. As he moved from barrel to barrel, his panic rose. Every single man and woman had perished. Not knowing what else to do, he fled Ali Baba's house. On seeing him depart, Morgiana finally went to bed.

The following morning, once the household had awoken, Morgiana told them of all she had done to protect their lives. Seeing the danger that he had brought upon not only his brother, but also every person he held dear, Ali Baba deeply regretted ever entering the cave that very first time. For her deeds, Morgiana was given her freedom, so that she was no longer a maid. And in truth Ali Baba was afraid not to do this, for now he saw the acts of which she was capable. From this moment onwards he would always live in fear, he realized. In fear of the captain of thieves, and even in fear of Morgiana in case she ever decided to call upon him. And though he still had the gold that he had taken from the cave that fateful day, Ali Baba now knew that the gold was not worth the price he had been forced to pay.

Vasilisa and Baba Yaga the Bony-Legged

In Slavic folklore, Baba Yaga is a being with magical powers. In some stories, for example the version found in Alexander Afanasyev's collection of tales titled *The Maiden Tsar*, she is one of three sisters who all share the same name. But in another telling, called "Vasilisa the Beautiful" and collected in Afanasyev's *Russian Fairy Tales*, there is just one Baba Yaga. This version published sometime between 1855 and 1863.

In a distant Tzardom, many miles from here, lived a girl called Vasilisa. Vasilisa was a lovely girl, as clever as she was kind. But sad things befall the lovely just as often as the loveless, and when Vasilisa was but eight years old, her mother became sick with an incurable illness. One night, when her mother felt sure that the end was near, she asked her daughter to come to her bedside. Holding her hand lightly, for by that time strength seemed to evade her, Vasilisa's mother handed her a small wooden doll. "Do not weep for me, dear child," she said, as the tears nonetheless fell down Vasilisa's cheeks, "but listen carefully to these words: though my time on this earth is almost over, I leave to you this small doll which my own mother once gave me. You must never show it to anyone, and you must always carry it with you, for, when you are in trouble or in need of comfort, the doll will help you. Even if you feel you have no one to turn to, remember this doll. Look after it, nurture it, feed it, and in turn the doll will do the same for you."

Vasilisa took the small doll in her hands and

promised her mother she would do exactly as she had said. Kissing her cheek for what would be the last time, Vasilisa held her mother's hand until the end came.

After her mother's death, Vasilisa was so overcome with grief that she forgot all about the doll. She missed her mother terribly and cried often, even in the night when she would wake from nightmares. On one such night, when Vasilisa reached under her pillow in search of a handkerchief with which to dry her eyes, she felt instead the shape of something else. It was the small wooden doll! At once remembering her mother's words, Vasilisa made her way to the pantry to find something for the doll to eat. As she held a piece of bread to the doll's face, she was amazed to see the doll's eyes brighten. Why, it was as if the doll had come alive! As the doll ate the bread, it told Vasilisa not to feel scared. "Everything appears worse at night-time," said the doll. "This is how it's always been. But lie down and sleep, for tomorrow you will feel a little bit better. Vasilisa took heed of the doll's words, and soon after going back to bed she fell into a deep and peaceful sleep. From that point onwards, Vasilisa fed the doll every day and found much comfort in the doll's presence, always keeping her close-by. And while she did still grieve for her mother, Vasilisa found that her grief started to become somewhat easier to bear.

Vasilisa's father was also grieving and, mistakenly feeling that he could not provide enough support for his daughter, he started looking for a new wife who would be able to look after Vasilisa in the ways he felt he could not. And so it was that he decided to marry a widow who herself had children – two daughters, of around the same age as Vasilisa. Vasilisa did not want a stepmother – or two stepsisters, for that matter – but she knew nothing of her father's true reason for remarrying, as he had not found the strength to speak to her about it. So Vasilisa kept her feelings a secret too, and instead decided to try her best to be a good daughter and stepdaughter. Unfortunately, her stepmother did not care to behave the same. Both she and her daughters treated Vasilisa terribly, making her do all of the work within the house and also sending her out to work in the fields, all the while doing no work themselves. They lived in a small house by the edge of a dark and ominous forest, and everyone who lived nearby – in fact all who lived for miles – knew that a fearsome witch by the name of Baba Yaga lived within the forest. It was rumoured that Baba Yaga ate whomever and whatever she came across within the woods, and so Vasilisa's stepmother would send her on errands in the hope that Baba Yaga would find her. Each time, however, Vasilisa would return home safely, having been guided by her wooden doll. This wasn't the only way Vasilisa's doll protected her. Whenever her stepmother or stepsisters were mean or dispiriting, Vasilisa's doll spoke encouraging words to her. No matter how little food Vasilisa was given, she always fed the doll and looked after it with care, and the doll did the same in return. There were times when her stepmother's behaviour made Vasilisa feel as if the world were against her, but in her heart Vasilisa knew that she always had her doll, and that gave her strength.

Years passed, and Vasilisa grew into a strong and determined young woman. The same could not be said for her stepmother and stepsisters, who remained horribly unkind and spiteful. And what of Vasilisa's father? He came and went as he pleased, spending weeks away from his family as he worked here or there. Perhaps he knew that Vasilisa was suffering, perhaps he chose not to see it. Either way, he was of no help to her. Vasilisa's stepmother had been thinking for a long time about how she could get rid of her stepdaughter. The girl's presence only made her feel bad: Vasilisa's goodness showed just how awful her stepmother was, and instead of making the woman want to be a better person, it filled her with jealousy and anger. She decided that there was no other option but to get rid of Vasilisa, in whatever way she could.

At first, Vasilisa's stepmother tried to make her leave with words. She felt that if she was mean enough to Vasilisa, then the girl would go. But Vasilisa found comfort in her doll, which she fed every day, and so was able to ignore much of what her stepmother said to her.

So her stepmother tried to make her leave by not giving her food. "We are so poor now," she said, "and there is very little to go around. You must be grateful for what you are given." Vasilisa received mere crusts of bread, while her stepsisters and stepmother ate everything they desired. Still, no matter how little she was given, Vasilisa always fed her doll first.

One evening, while Vasilisa's father was still away, her stepmother came up with a wicked idea that would surely rid her of her stepdaughter once and for all. Hiding their candles and putting out the fire, she called Vasilisa. "My dearest stepdaughter," she said, in a tone that was unsettling to Vasilisa, as she was quite unused to her stepmother speaking to her kindly. "We seem to have no way of making light and warmth, and I was told tonight would be a cold night indeed. Please, go to Baba Yaga and ask for some fire." At once Vasilisa realized what her stepmother was doing – she wished to send Vasilisa into the forest to suffer death at the witch's hands. But as much as Vasilisa tried to protest, her stepmother would not give up. Finally, Vasilisa was forced to pack a bag and set off into the forest to find Baba Yaga.

Trembling with fear, Vasilisa walked deeper into the forest. But she held her little wooden doll tightly and was much comforted by its words. "Do not fear, Vasilisa," it said, "for I will keep you safe from harm." With her confidence bolstered, Vasilisa continued on her way to Baba Yaga's abode. On she went, through the night, and the darkness seemed to close in on her. All of a sudden, Vasilisa heard the thundering of hooves as a horseman galloped past her at speed. He was dressed entirely in white, and his steed was also white. As he passed, the first silver rays of dawn appeared in the sky. Some time later, Vasilisa heard the sound of hooves once more, as another horseman galloped past her. This time he was dressed in red and rode upon a red steed. As he galloped past, the sun started to rise, shining light upon the topmost branches of the trees.

Vasilisa walked all day, not really knowing where she was going. There was no path in the forest, and no one knew how to find Baba Yaga, for all they ever really wanted was to stay well away from her. There were rumours that her house was made of magic and that it moved from place to place. Just as Vasilisa was starting to feel as if she may not be able to take another step, she noticed a clearing within the trees. There she saw a small hut, but, as she walked towards it, she was startled to see that it was moving – indeed, it was spinning around and around. Was she dreaming? Walking closer still, Vasilisa saw that the curious hut was standing upon chickens' legs. There was a fence around it that was made of bones, and on the top of each bone a skull was placed. The holes where eyes had once been seemed to stare at Vasilisa intently, as if telling her to turn around and flee. The fence led to a gate, which Vasilisa saw had hands for hinges, and the lock was a jawbone with sharp iron teeth set within it. At the mere sight of this monstrosity, Vasilisa's blood ran cold. She was rooted to the spot with fear.

The sound of a third set of hooves broke Vasilisa's concentration and she looked up to see a third horseman, this one dressed in black and riding upon a black steed. He galloped up to the gate before which Vasilisa stood, and as his steed leapt towards the hut, both the horse and its rider disappeared into thin air. At the very same moment, night fell across the forest as if a black blanket had been placed over every living thing. As it did so, the eye sockets within each skull lit up, casting a sinister light amongst the trees, and the forest started to make the most frightening noises. The trees groaned, the branches creaked, the leaves rustled, and Vasilisa realized with great fear that in the distance she could see Baba Yaga crashing through the shrub. Standing within her giant iron mortar, clutching her pestle within one of her bony hands, Baba Yaga looked fearsome indeed. Through the undergrowth she blazed, clearing the trail left behind her by brushing it with an enormous broom that she grasped in her other hand. Within moments she had reached the gate, and when she did so the hut that stood spinning before Vasilisa immediately stilled. Baba

Yaga's nose flew into the air as she smelled around her, and to Vasilisa's horror, the witch looked about her with beady eyes. "I do believe I smell Russian bones!" she cried, in a voice that Vasilisa was sure could curdle milk. "Who's there? Who's there, I say!" Stepping out of the shadows, Vasilisa composed herself to speak.

"It is I," she said. "Vasilisa. I come asking for your help. Please, can you help me obtain fire for light and warmth?"

Baba Yaga considered the girl before her with much interest, and even sniffed the air around her again before leaning further over her mortar to speak to her again. "Have you come of your own free will, or were you sent?" she asked. "My stepmother sent me," said Vasilisa, and Baba Yaga nodded in reply. "Your stepmother, yes," muttered the witch. "I know her, indeed I do." After a moment's pause, the gate protecting Baba Yaga's horrifying house swung open, surprising Vasilisa and making her jump back in fear. "I will give you fire," shouted Baba Yaga, "but you must work for it. And if you do not work for it then I shall eat you up. Do you agree?" Vasilisa did agree, for she knew not what else to do, and no sooner had she done so than did the wind start howling in the most dreadful manner, whistling so loudly that Vasilisa feared her eardrums might burst. Into her garden rode Baba Yaga, with Vasilisa following, and the gate crashed shut behind them.

Once inside, the witch noisily sat herself down at the table. "Take everything out of the oven and put it here," she said, pointing at the table in front of her. "Hurry up!" she shouted, while Vasilisa looked around the room in a panic. She didn't even know where the oven was. As soon as she spotted it, she rushed forward and carefully withdrew the piping-hot dishes from within. There was enough food to feed at least a dozen people, but the witch started eating it with such gusto that Vasilisa had no doubt it would all be gone soon enough. "Fetch me a drink," called Baba Yaga, with a full mouth, "and be quick about it." This Vasilisa did, and when she brought it to the table she was stunned by the mess the woman had made in such a small space of time: chicken bones already lay sprawled across the table, and when the witch came across a gristly bit, she simply spat it out, not caring where it went. When she had at last finished eating, she picked up a very small piece of bread. "You may have this," she said, passing it to Vasilisa as she mopped grease from her chin with her other hand, "and listen to me closely. Tomorrow you must clean my house from top to bottom, weed my garden and cook for me. When that is done, you must take all of the wheat from my storehouse and pick every bad grain from the store. Do not miss even one bad grain, or I will eat you for my supper."

With that, Baba Yaga took her leave and went to bed, leaving Vasilisa to sleep by the fire. When the terrible woman had gone, Vasilisa sat down and removed her little wooden doll from her pocket. "Eat up, little doll," she said, as she shared her bread with it, "and please hear my words. I fear I have done the wrong thing, and now I am trapped here with a terrible witch who wants to eat me." But the doll spoke softly to Vasilisa, and made her feel much calmed. "Try to sleep, dear Vasilisa," it said, "and fear not, for I will take care of you." Vasilisa fell asleep almost immediately.

When she awoke the next morning, it was still dark outside. Vasilisa could hear Baba Yaga crashing around within the house, and as Vasilisa looked out of the window she saw the white horseman race past the hut, bringing with him the early morning light. Past Vasilisa the witch went, making her way outside and into her giant iron mortar. As she did so, Vasilisa saw the red horseman ride past, bringing with him the first rays of sunshine that day. Baba Yaga was now ready to leave, and she called out magic words which opened the gate before her. The earth shook and the trees groaned, and leaves whirled about her in a truly terrifying fashion. No sooner had the gate opened but did Baba Yaga bluster through it, and though Vasilisa did try to escape through the gate too, it flew shut so quickly that she simply wasn't quick enough. In the distance, she heard Baba Yaga's cackling laugh.

Knowing that there was no way to escape, Vasilisa set to work, starting the chores that Baba Yaga had instructed her to do. She was used to hard work, and she found that being busy made the fear of her imprisonment go away a little bit. But still, it took Vasilisa so long to clean Baba Yaga's house and cook for her that by the time she heard the screeching witch returning, she hadn't even had the time to step foot outside the house. *Oh no!* she thought with fear. *I've not weeded the garden or even started to separate the good wheat from the bad. The witch is certain to eat me now.* She cowered inside, waiting for the witch to enter. When she did, she looked about the room in surprise. "I can see you've cleaned," she said, "and I can smell that you've cooked," she added, with her nose in the air. "I also saw that you weeded my garden," the witch said, which surprised Vasilisa enormously. Following Baba Yaga outside, Vasilisa saw that the garden was now neat and tidy, with not one weed to be seen. Putting her hand in her pocket, she felt her small wooden doll and knew that the doll had helped her so. Leading Vasilisa to the grain store, the witch looked about the room and shouted out in shock at what she saw. "You have finished all of the work!" she said. Sure enough, when Vasilisa looked into the room she saw that all of the good grain had been separated from the bad. Curiously, the witch shouted out more magic words and three pairs of hands appeared from nowhere. "Take the wheat for grinding!" Baba Yaga commanded, and the hands seized the wheat and took it away – every last good grain.

Begrudgingly, the witch finally went back inside and sat down at the table for dinner.

"You have done well," she told Vasilisa, "but before I give you light you must do it all again tomorrow. You must clean the house, weed the garden, cook my food and then…" At this the witch paused to consider what impossible task she should choose. "Take all of the poppy seeds from my stores," she continued, with a wicked look on her face. "Each seed is covered in dirt. I want you to clean every single one so that not a speck of dirt remains."

When the witch had gone to sleep, Vasilisa took her doll from her pocket to share with it the crust of bread she had been given. "Thank you, dear doll, thank you," said Vasilisa. For she knew that had it not been for the doll's help, Baba Yaga would have eaten her that day. The doll hushed Vasilisa to sleep, telling her that she would do all she could to help her and keep her safe.

The next morning, Vasilisa woke to an ear-splitting whistle outside and rushed to the door just in time to see Baba Yaga fly off in her giant mortar. Straight away Vasilisa set to work inside the house, cleaning and tidying, and cooking an enormous meal for the witch. And just as the doll had helped her the day before, so it did that day as well, weeding the garden that had somehow grown overnight, and setting to work cleaning the poppy seeds as the witch had instructed. After some hours, Vasilisa and her doll had finished all of the tasks demanded of them. As she looked back out of the window, Vasilisa saw the black horseman riding up to the gates and disappearing like a shadow. Darkness fell once more across the forest. Soon Baba Yaga would return. As the house started to shake, Vasilisa knew that moment had arrived, and the ground shook as Baba Yaga burst in through the door. This time she uttered no word but immediately set about the house, checking on Vasilisa's work, before blustering outside to look at the garden and check the poppy seeds. Baba Yaga inspected the seeds with disappointment, seeing clearly that she had no reason to force Vasilisa to stay there any longer. Then she clapped her hands, and at once the three pairs of hands reappeared and took the poppy seeds away.

Sitting down at the table, Baba Yaga waited for Vasilisa to serve her the abundance of food she had prepared. Plate by plate, bowl by bowl, Vasilisa filled the table and Baba Yaga tucked in greedily. When she noticed Vasilisa watching her, the witch put down a large piece of meat she had been feasting on. "What is it?" she shouted, as juice dripped down her chin. "With your permission," Vasilisa replied, "I would like to ask you some questions." "Very well," said Baba Yaga, "but just remember that not all questions lead to good. If you know too much you become old too soon. Go on then, ask!"

"I would like to ask you about the horsemen," said Vasilisa. "Who was the man in white who rode past me in the forest?"

"That was the dawn," answered Baba Yaga, grinding her teeth.

"And who was the red horseman?" asked Vasilisa.

"That was the sun," answered Baba Yaga, gnashing her teeth loudly. She was scaring Vasilisa somewhat, but the girl decided to continue.

"Who was the black horseman?" she asked, as the witch's eyes flashed fiercely.

"That was the night," replied the witch, who was shouting at this point. "And do you have any other questions, girl?" she shrieked.

Vasilisa thought of the three pairs of hands that had magically appeared and disappeared, and was about to ask the witch about them but quickly stopped herself when she saw the vicious look in the witch's eyes.

"Well?" Baba Yaga demanded. "You must have more questions?" But Vasilisa said nothing. "Ask me another question!" shrieked the witch. But Vasilisa shook her head. "Three questions are enough for me," she said with care. "After all, I do not want to become old too soon. As you said, not every question leads to good."

Baba Yaga snarled with annoyance. "It is just as well. Those who ask questions about things they see outside of the fence will get an answer. But those who ask questions about things that happen within do not live to see another day. And now I have a question for you. How is it that you have been able to finish all of the work I asked of you? It should have been an impossible task!"

By this point, Vasilisa was terrified by the witch's anger, but she still managed to whisper a reply. "My mother's love helped me," she said. Immediately Baba Yaga sprung up, filled with rage. "Get out!" she cried. "Get out! I will have no mother's love here!"

Vasilisa ran out of the house, standing on its peculiar chicken legs, and through the garden. Hearing Baba Yaga's voice behind her, she saw the gate fly open to allow her passage, the lock opening with a loud *snick!* But before she could pass through the gate, Baba Yaga jumped before Vasilisa. Taking a skull from the fence that surrounded her house, the witch passed it to the girl. "Give this to your stepmother," she spat, before rushing back into her house.

With the glowing skull lighting her way, Vasilisa started her journey home. All night she walked, not stopping once for fear that the witch would come after her. After many hours, the glowing eyes within the skull flickered and went out. Moments later, Vasilisa heard the sound of hooves behind her, and turned to see the white horseman gallop past. In the distance, the sky started to lighten. Soon after, the red horseman galloped past, and Vasilisa noticed sunlight touching the uppermost tips of the trees as the sun started to climb in the sky. All day she walked, until it was time for day to turn into night. To her surprise, when Vasilisa looked down at the skull she still held, she saw the eyes flicker and start to glow again. Just then there was a thundering of hooves as the black horseman galloped past and the forest was thrown into darkness once more. On Vasilisa walked until finally she saw her father's small cottage up ahead. With a great sigh of relief, she walked the final few steps, but as she neared the place she was surprised to see that there was no light on – not inside or out. Walking into the house, Vasilisa saw her stepmother and stepsisters sitting in darkness. Ever since she had gone, they said, there had been no light in the house. Whenever they tried to light a candle or the fire, it would immediately go out. They hadn't even been able to eat. They were shocked to see Vasilisa come home, but even more shocked to see that she brought fire with her. Grasping at it greedily, her stepsisters and stepmother seemed mesmerized, wanting the fire for themselves. But when they touched it something strange happened; the skull seemed to flash hot-white, its eyes boring into them until the three women – the stepmother and both stepsisters – were burnt to ashes. Only Vasilisa was untouched by the skull's mystical powers. The next morning she dug a hole in the ground and carefully buried the skull. Her father never returned, but Vasilisa lived in the cottage for the rest of her days and always remembered the time she had come face-to-face with Baba Yaga.

Now discover another selection of enchanting tales...

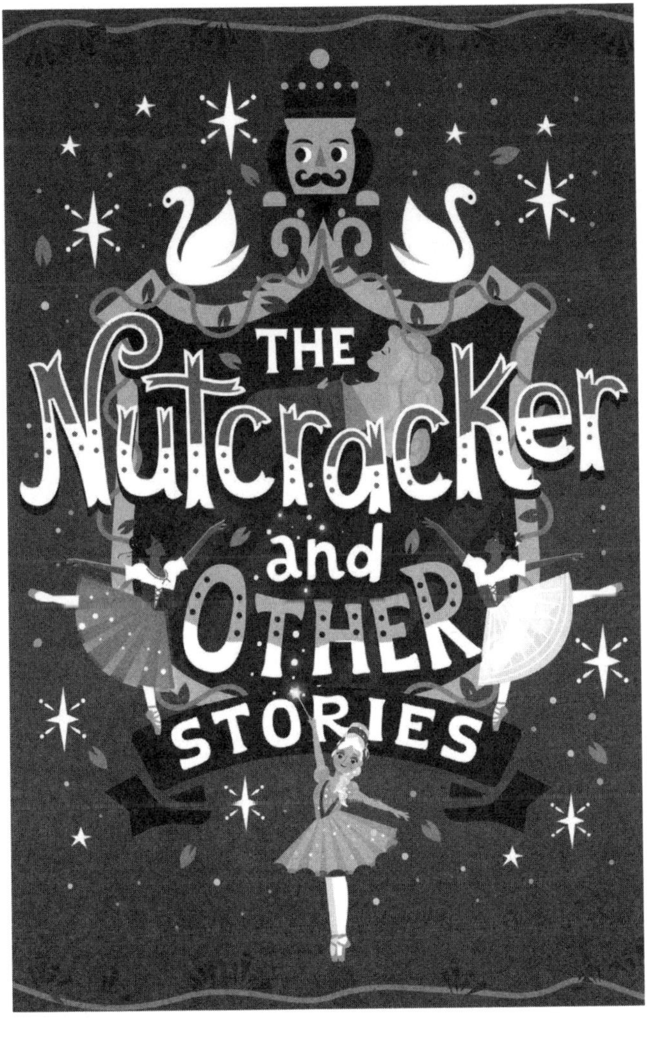